Advance Praise for
Made in China

"A fun and fascinating look at the intricacies of Chinese traditions surrounding pregnancy and birth, from nutrition to numerology. Simon Gjeroe offers a friendly helping hand to other foreigners attempting, like him, to navigate a path through a landscape of often perplexing cultural differences."
—Fuchsia Dunlop, author of *Shark's Fin and Sichuan Pepper: A Sweet-Sour Memoir of Eating in China*

"A must-read for any parent-to-be, no matter where they are in the world. Part manual, part memoir, this rich tale of fatherhood captures the wonderful, fascinating otherness of raising a baby in a culture outside of one's own."
—Tom O'Malley, author of *Beijing Lonely Planet 12th Edition*

"A delight to read. In amongst all the tomes seeking to deep dive China, Simon Gjero's is a refreshingly honest account of one of the most singular experiences in any culture–making, birthing and raising babies."
—Paul French, author of *Midnight in Peking*

MADE IN CHINA

A Memoir of Marriage and Mixed Babies in the Middle Kingdom

Simon Gjeroe

Made in China

By Simon Gjeroe

ISBN-13: 978-988-8769-19-3

© 2020 Simon Gjeroe

Illustrations by Ina Korneliussen

This book has been reset in 10pt Book Antiqua. Spellings and punctuations are left as in the original edition.

BIOGRAPHY & AUTOBIOGRAPHY

EB 139

All rights reserved. No part of this book may be reproduced in material form, by any means, whether graphic, electronic, mechanical or other, including photocopying or information storage, in whole or in part. May not be used to prepare other publications without written permission from the publisher except in the case of brief quotations embodied in critical articles or reviews. For information contact info@earnshawbooks.com

Published by Earnshaw Books Ltd. (Hong Kong)

To Fu, Luka, Louis and Anna

This work depicts actual events in the life of the author as truthfully as recollection permits. As love, life and parenthood in a foreign culture is a serious business, the names and details of some people have been changed to respect their privacy and marital bliss.

Contents

1. What's going on? — 1
2. I kissed the teacher — 16
3. What does she want? — 28
4. If I had a million dollars — 39
5. I couldn't help but notice — 44
6. Teach me tiger — 49
7. Blue or pink? — 63
8. Happy Birthday — 76
9. The Eagle has landed — 81
10. Blond or black? — 97
11. What's in a name? — 101
12. Re-education through labour — 113
13. Xiao Hello! — 130
14. A small step forward — 141
15. To be or not to be — 147
16. Fifty Shades — 158
17. Who's who? — 164
18. No time for losers — 170
19. Under the Influence — 180
20. The Long March — 186
Epilogue: Made in Denmark — 192

1

What's going on?

GETTING MARRIED in China can be a breath-taking, memorable and hopefully also a lifelong cultural experience, but my first Chinese wedding experience was not my own.

Patrick, my French-Canadian roommate in Sichuan University, in early 1996, was marrying the love of his life, a sweet local girl, and I was invited. Also invited were my friends Sasha from Vladivostok and fellow Russian roommate Pasha, who were the godfathers of the foreign students dormitory, and Radek from Poland. They were a jolly bunch and skilled in the art of heavy drinking, but also took their time in the local university gym very seriously, and certainly looked the part too. After leaving our *hongbao* (red envelopes containing newly-printed cash that was immediately counted and registered) out front, we grabbed some of the sweets and cigarettes on offer (many of the Chinese guests put the cigarettes behind their ears), and then, together with Sasha's American girlfriend, Jennifer, were politely shown to our table. It was in a giant hotel ballroom with about a couple of hundred guests, and as the only foreigners, and as such treated as guests of honour, we were sitting right in front of the red silk-clad happy couple and the bride's parents.

The Chinese students at Sichuan University called our drab, three-story building surrounded by a high wall with broken glass on top, the 'Panda Building', apparently because we were better protected than China's most famous and cutest animal. Being rare and precious, I'd say we got at least as much attention at the party as the bridal couple.

After the obligatory tea ceremony where the couple bowed three times in front of her parents, it seems to me that every Chinese male in the room started to queue up in front of us. They saw it as their polite obligation to toast the foreign guests, and so they did, several times over. While I vividly remember the hundreds of anonymous people standing in line before me and the clear, strong Chinese liquor known as *baijiu* (pronounced "bye Joe") that was thrown down with each toast, I remember almost nothing about the food, apart from the fact that it was an incredibly spicy hot pot. The succession of red faces quickly became a blur as the toasts came faster and faster. Also the alcohol-soaked table and the slippery floor, because many of the toasters, simply took the easy way out. I noticed that aspect just a little bit too late. When I finally collapsed in the Panda Building, I remember thinking that it had all happened at a trailblazing speed, the whole thing was over in just a couple of hours.

Although the many local Chinese traditions are definitely an important and fun part of getting married here, still tasting the Sichuanese *baijiu* even several days later during continuous and vicious hiccups, this was definitely not how I envisioned my own wedding.

I can't help but consider myself luckier than Patrick, as Fu and I, on the first Saturday in December 2008, celebrated our betrothal with a relatively small gathering of family and friends. Fu, wore a stunning red silk wedding dress and I stood by the door passing out candy and cigarettes to the thirty some people we had invited. On the way in, many congratulated us with a

WHAT'S GOING ON?

"*baitou xielao*", to live together until the white hairs of old age, which I learned is a common blessing for Chinese newlyweds. Apart from Fu's cousins who were apparently very hungry, no one was in a rush. Underneath the Chinese character for double happiness 囍, which is exclusively used for weddings, we had magnificent Sichuanese and Guangdong cuisine at a restaurant (more than four stars as the well-trained and beautiful young waitress repeatedly told us) managed by my brother-in-law, but owned by the air force and normally off-limits to foreigners. The fine red Bordeaux was not accompanied by any *baijiu* (in time, I learned to appreciate the finer nuances of the best-selling liquor in the world), but rather by huge glasses of peanut milk, not altogether a bad combination, but mostly because Fu and many of her family members would have been knocked to the ground with even the smallest amount of alcohol. It is a condition caused by an inherited deficiency in one of the enzymes involved in the breakdown of alcohol and results in almost immediate nausea, sweating, headache, racing heart, dizziness, along with facial flushing. It's often called Asian flush or Asian glow, and it's very common in East Asia.

While the majority of our guests spent the afternoon enjoying themselves drinking green tea, smoking and playing *mahjong*, which looks like dominoes but has rules similar to the card game Rummy, I have to admit that Fu and I sneaked out for a cup of Starbucks coffee. However, one of the benefits of being in a mixed Chinese-foreigner relationship is that most of us are going to have another wedding party at a later date.

In Chinese, how to say "to marry..." is gender specific. For women, Chinese use the character 嫁 (*jia*), comprising of 'woman' and 'family', which basically means that she will enter the man's family. For men, they use 娶 (*qu*), comprising of 'woman' and 'to take', which clearly indicates what will happen. Traditionally, in China, the groom's family pays for the entire wedding, and also have to deliver an apartment, a car (with parking space) and preferably both a PhD and a Beijing or Shanghai hukou–the Chinese household registration system that fixes people in their place, and which can be described as a modern form of serfdom. And that is just to get started! I know you should follow the lead of those who know the ropes, but still. Author of *Leftover in China*, Roseann Lake wrote "Basically, marriage in China has the equivalent social force of a steamroller. It's simply what one does."

We since went to many weddings in China and witnessed many both fun and romantic traditions and ceremonies, but often we felt that the bridal couple had no idea what they signified and why they were necessary. And that, most often, at a trailblazing speed that left even the 'Fast and Furious' movies looking slow. It was also frequently a fascinating cocktail of both Chinese and Western traditions, all orchestrated by an unknown toastmaster, working against the clock, fitting in as many traditions (real or invented) to the shortest amount of time possible.

The day before, we had shown up at a local government office whose sole task in this world is to marry or divorce Chinese citizens who are in relationships with foreigners. The cost of a marriage was sixteen yuan (about US$2.50), while a divorce cost close to half that at nine yuan. After entering what could best be described as an anonymous lobby in a nondescript, dull, ten-floor toilet-style Chinese office building plastered with drab whitish tiles and blue or black-tinted windows, a skinny office clerk in his late twenties approached us with a straight, slightly nervous expression.

"Are you getting married or filing for a divorce?" he asked.

We replied "marriage", and his face lit up. He invited us to step inside and take out all the necessary documents. It had been next to impossible to find out exactly which documents we needed to bring, except my certificate of marriageability issued, translated and stamped by the Danish Embassy, so we were quite nervous. Some friends had even had to provide a letter from the parents of the Chinese partner including the fingerprints of both parents, giving permission for their daughter to marry a foreigner. Until 2003, it was mandatory to have a pre-marital check-up at the hospital to ask about tobacco and alcohol habits, check for venereal diseases as well as for leprosy, mental disorders, and other hereditary diseases, and to make sure that the future bride was a virgin. Afterwards, you also had to sit for a movie or talk about the use of contraceptives and how to make babies. I read in a local newspaper about a Chinese couple who, according to doctors' orders, literally had 'slept together' for several years, but couldn't understand why she was not getting pregnant. Now it was voluntary.

I would have liked to sit for the talk as it could have been fun, but then a slightly intimidating, heavy-set woman in her late forties, powerfully built with broad shoulders and with her black hair pulled sternly away from her face and rolled into a tight twist at the back of her head, stepped out, pointing stringently at the time. Even though it was only 10 am and the office was, except for us, absolutely empty, she glanced worriedly at the big clock in the hall, and asked us to come back after 1 pm, because she was afraid that we would infringe upon their two-hour lunch break.

Fair enough, this is China, and if there is one thing you quickly learn, it is that midday meal times (and the subsequent nap) are almost sacred. Having said that, we were apparently in luck that day because upon our return in the afternoon (after a visit to Fu's favourite local restaurant which probably makes the best spicy noodles east of the Himalayas), after being interviewed by the clerk who meticulously dotted all the i's and crossed all the t's, and after receiving dozens of stamps here, there and everywhere on the documents, we were cordially married. Just like that, it was over. A little bit too quickly, with no ceremony, and not really what Fu or I had in mind when thinking of such a huge and important occasion in our lives. To make it a little romantic, I got down on one knee, looked Fu in the eyes and put the ring on her finger. We kissed and that was that. Later we went to one of the cosy teahouses in the peaceful Wenshu Monastery, dating back to the Tang dynasty, and in the evening went for great spicy Sichuan food with a few good friends.

Now newly-wedded, we went for a short honeymoon at a small mountain spa outside Chengdu, where we were the only guests in a rather deserted hotel. A few days later, we flew back to Beijing, where I made sure to carry my bride in through our rather narrow front door. According to Chinese beliefs, it should have been over a pan of burning coals to ensure a trouble-free labour in the event of a future pregnancy, but we were out of coal and the BBQ had been put away for the winter.

Many Chinese couples perform the official marriage registration months or even years before they embark on any kind of celebration. Many also go through very elaborate wedding photo sessions in picturesque or "exotic" locations such as in front of Christian churches and other Western-style buildings, even way before they actually get married. I just love to watch the happy couples lining up, often half a dozen at the same time, each with their own entourage, for their individual shoots, which often take the better part of a whole day, and involving numerous rented outfits both Western and Chinese-style, and sometimes even include bridesmaids. It's fun to see that, when the bride lifts up her shining white wedding dress to actually be able to walk, you can often see that underneath she

WHAT'S GOING ON?

is wearing a pair of sneakers, and, in season, woollen long johns. The photo shoots are a little like getting a memory of something which has not yet taken place.

For us, this all happened on two typically damp, cold and misty Sichuan December days in 2008. It was a year of great significance for not only Fu and I, but also for China. It was the year of the Beijing Olympics in August, preceded by inescapable countdown clocks, and massive destruction of Beijing's age-old houses and neighborhoods with the whole world watching. The change of pace in Beijing was overwhelming, but fitted very well with the Olympic slogan "Faster, Higher, Stronger". The American journalist, Alex Pasternack described it really well when he wrote: "It all happened so quickly that there wasn't much time to consider what had been erased. Just time to get in (an orderly) line, move on (or move out to the suburbs), and stare slack-jawed at what replaced it all." We lived through it all, and even survived as a couple even though Fu was close to being thrown out of Beijing ahead of the Olympics because, at the time, God forbid it, we were living together without being married.

We made up for the lack of a romantic ceremony, and the absence of sun and warmth on our wedding day when, half a year later, on a beautiful Beijing Saturday in May, surrounded by our family and close friends, with nearly a hundred guests in all present, our marriage was blessed by a Danish priest. It took place near the old Drum Tower, in a charming Beijing rustic courtyard dating back centuries, which was covered in purple flowers from a large wisteria vine climbing up to lend shadow to where we were kneeling. As the wisteria symbolizes both love, reverence and longevity, it could hardly have been more romantic. It was a spine-tingling moment to cherish for life, and we had the most beautiful evening with delicious light and sophisticated spicy cuisine from the multi-ethnic province of Yunnan in southwest

China, which we both love, and a Mongolian band played their rhythmic music accompanied by the characteristic throat singing that we had come to cherish so much. In the afternoon we took all the hundred guests for a successful publicity stunt, when we lined them up in front of the little shop my friend Lars Ulrik and I had opened just months before in the nearby popular Nanluogu Alley, selling historic maps of Beijing and China and old-school black and white postcards. Drawn by the crowds, Chinese and other tourists quickly started lining up as well. All in all, it was a great day and a perfect mix of Chinese and Danish traditions, the party continuing on to the early hours of Sunday morning, when the Chinese neighbors, understandably, wearing their pyjamas and slippers started coming, looking less happy about the music and noise. The only spoiler was that a few weeks before I had broken my right foot in a football game, so I was wearing my black suit on top of an oversized and ugly grey walking boot, and, not least, the fact that Fu couldn't hide the baby bump on her milky white and later (after changing) red silk wedding dress.

The first time I really started to consider my life as a prospective father was when I was around twenty-two or twenty-three years old. One day, as I was staying in a small village in the southern province of Guangxi, I chanced upon an old soothsayer from the Yi ethnic minority who I still remember vividly. She stood only about 1.5 meters (less than five feet) tall, had more wrinkles than a Chinese Shar-pei puppy, and only a few crooked teeth left in her mouth, all stained a reddish-black, dyed from years of chewing betel nuts. She wore a big black turban with her white hair sticking out, and a cape over a simple blue and reddish set of clothes. Around her neck, dangling from her long earlobes, and wrapped around her wrists were elaborate and lovely pieces

WHAT'S GOING ON?

of silver jewelry. I believe (maybe naively) that I was the first foreigner she had ever set her beady black eyes on. She looked directly at me for a while and then took my left hand and turned it over and looked at my palm with a concentrated look on her face. Then she started to tell me what my future would be. Maybe because of the betel in her mouth or because she spoke only limited and broken Chinese, and my Chinese was very far from perfect at the time, I did not understand that much. However, what I did understand was that I would live to be 88 years old, and father no less than four children. After she finished predicting my future, almost to underscore her divination, she spat a red chunk of saliva on the ground dangerously close to my feet and left.

Fu and I had been trying for children for some months (Fu had long since given up smoking), even before we were married (please don't tell anyone), but since nothing had really happened and considering we were both already in our mid-thirties, we began to wonder if everything was okay down there. This included me visiting a very local hospital to have 'my everything' looked at thoroughly, while struggling to keep the door closed to prevent people from peeking in. Ultimately, I was prescribed something probably derived from a poor dead animal or a fast-disappearing exotic forest somewhere in Southeast Asia. It wasn't fair on my little boys to stand trial on such a hot and humid August day in Beijing anyway.

Then I did what probably quite a few Chinese, but very few foreigners, would consider normal. I invited a couple of friends out for a meal at the local restaurant called *Guolizhuang*, which translates into something like "the contents of the pot will make you strong". Here we were shown into a small private room for a dinner consisting of mainly animal genitalia, which, according to

Chinese beliefs, should increase male potency. To be more precise, a set menu which had been given the poetic name "The Essence of the Golden Buddha" was presented to us and it included not only ox, sheep and dog penis and testicles, but also a floating turtle and a sprinkle of seahorses. To my surprise, it was really tasty, although the dog penises were a little like eating a really old gummy bear. The waitress politely explained that our female companion should avoid eating the testicles, because it could give her both a deeper voice and even a beard. But she added that the penises would be fine for her to eat. Harmless or not, I have to say that I was very sceptical to begin with, but I must admit that for the next twenty-four hours after we had finished our exotic meal, I have never felt so energized. I might sound weird, but I really felt like a ball of pure energy was streaming out from my belly and through my whole body. Animal genitalia or exotic forest plants, whatever the reason, something happened down there and just one month after our December wedding, Fu came to me one day with the delightful, but shocking news that she was pregnant.

I quickly realized that being "pregnant" (as I find so many men say nowadays) in China was very different from what I had learned from friends back in Denmark, or indeed any other country I can think of. Surely 99% of all books on pregnancy in any language have been written for women (fair enough), but I found myself needing answers too, as a whole string of mysterious local China-based phenomena emerged. My wife and I suddenly became the responsibility of a whole nation, access to my bedroom was denied because I was born in the year of the tiger, sales assistants refused to sell my wife knickers, complete strangers told her what she should and should not wear and eat, while others would cross the street with the sole purpose

WHAT'S GOING ON?

of staring at the shape of my wife's growing belly and predict the gender of the baby. I tried to find information online and in books, but found it pretty much absent altogether.

So what does a foreign man do in China when he is a father-to-be? I had thought, obviously naively, that cultural differences wouldn't be a cause for concern. It was "just" a pregnancy, something millions of fathers all around the world go through every year. How hard could it be? What do other guys do? They buy a (simple) book. Who needs a manual? And although books for fathers are not as rare as they used to be, they are still not readily available. It can be a daunting task to look into the many books your wife may have brought home on the second day, simply because, first of all most of them are thicker than the Bible (and will be read like one too), and secondly you would need a medical dictionary to understand them. And if that was not enough, they are all in Chinese! And have you noticed how most men like to think we can figure things out as we go along, never admitting that we're completely lost, and certainly won't give in by asking for directions? And let me tell you, there were countless times when I definitely could have used a GPS. The numerous cultural challenges I have faced in China while becoming a father have often left me feeling curious, sometimes delighted, once in a while very annoyed, and quite honestly a little lost at times.

Would you know the answer to questions like, "Can we do any housework during the pregnancy?" "Can we have sex or even sleep together during pregnancy?", "How to behave when complete strangers come up to you, stare up and down at you wife, even feel her stomach and tell her what to and what not to wear?", "Where can you go and who can you visit during the pregnancy?", "Can you take your wife seriously if she starts to wear overalls with teddy bears or oversized dresses looking like an X-ray apron from the local hospital?", "What to eat and not to eat during and after the pregnancy?", "Can you live with your wife if she has not showered for a month after the delivery?", "Will my parents-in-law move in with us?", "Do I have to eat the placenta?", "How come nobody comes to visit after the child is born?", "What is *kaidangku*?" etc. etc. And this is just to get started. Not surprisingly this can result in the need to scream out at the top of the lungs: "What's going on?"

This is the book trying to find out what's actually going on.

Before I spill the beans, I have to mention that the Chinese have a saying that if the vessel is full of water it does not make a sound, but if it's only half full it makes a lot of noise. "*Man guan shui bu xiang, ban guan xiang dingdang*" is the Chinese equivalent of the proverb "Empty vessels make the most noise".

In other words, when I had spent six months in China, as a twenty-year-old, I knew everything there was to know about the country. After having spent more than twenty years working with China, I am not so sure anymore. Confucius puts it this way "Real knowledge is to know the extent of one's ignorance". The American China expert and former professor at Berkeley, Orville Schell who has been working with and reporting from China for five decades, says it perfectly:

"Truthfully, I don't know where things are going. In China, things are always going in opposite directions at the same time. And there is no understanding the place, unless you can embrace such contradictions in your head at the same time."

This is exactly how I feel.

Nevertheless, let's start with some simple math. If you, and especially your wife, have good medical insurance, then you shouldn't have any problems here. Unfortunately, this wasn't the case for me, even though I should have known better after having

WHAT'S GOING ON?

worked for a number of years in the expat insurance business in China. I found myself needing to find a lump sum of money equivalent to buying a small used car (or a new Chinese-made and eco-friendly, electric Chery eQ), or around two thousand Tsingtao beers in a local bar, and I only had nine months to get it.

Quite early on in Fu's pregnancy, I discovered that things were quite different in China. And why, of course, wouldn't they be? Since I hadn't seen anyone else write about their experience of becoming a father in China, I thought to myself: why not try and write some articles about the whole situation? Apart from anything else, it would be fun for our child to read it all one day. So that's exactly what I did, and the series of articles entitled "Made in China" about the pregnancy itself, followed by a sequel under the title "Made in China 2" about the first six months after our first son Luka was born, were published in Denmark, Norway, the UK, Germany, Australia, and China and eventually helped to fund nearly half the cost of the first delivery.

After many friends and acquaintances started to ask me to share many of my personal experiences, I decided to collate all of these experiences into a small book for the benefit of many more people both in China and around the world. And here it is.

I have found one rather funny book about becoming a father written by a Danish TV and radio host, but even though he is spot-on with regard to many situations and has taught me what a giraffe says (or doesn't for that matter), which is important to know when you start looking at picture books with your children, nothing prepared me for the full package of cultural experiences and challenges in China.

On a practical level, this book will hopefully be of some use for the millions who find their loved one, marry and have children with someone from another culture. And specifically for the thousands of foreigners who marry the love of their life, who just happens to come from China or is of Chinese descent, and for whom the wonderful world of pregnancy and parenthood lies ahead. But above all, no matter the country, my goal here is to tell a hopefully funny, fascinating and heart-warming story about the human race and the most fundamental of all things -- life!

It's based on my experiences with my lovely wife Fu, and our two wonderful sons, Luka and Louis, together with stories and anecdotes from China-based friends and acquaintances. But before I go any deeper, it is probably wise to add some sort of a disclaimer here. Just as every woman is different, so is every pregnancy, and as China is a huge country with around 1.4 billion people and significant cultural differences between the north, south, east and west, and between countryside and city, you might not experience all the same cultural challenges and shocks that I have, but I am sure you will be faced with at least some of them. And maybe different ones entirely. Equally, you might find very similar or identical taboos, superstitions and old wives tales in other cultures as well.

I am not trying to write a book to point fingers or to compare every cultural difference, I'm just writing about my own experiences of becoming a father in China. It's difficult to say what is right and what is wrong. Just remember that even though you might not think a certain custom is right, one-fourth of the world's population, that is, most Chinese, might think otherwise. By way of example, consider plastic gloves and hot orange juice with your set meal at a local Chinese burger joint, or drinking boiling water when it is 40 degrees Celsius outside. That being said, it's important to say that, although I do try my best, I think that to always be the very sympathetic and understanding observer, is honestly quite difficult. Living in China, like being an expat anywhere else in the world, where

WHAT'S GOING ON?

cultures are so fundamentally different, can really be a love-hate relationship. Whether or not men are from Mars and women are from Venus or vice-versa (or if women aren't even from this solar system, a frustrated and slightly drunk friend once philosophized), the truth is, let's face it, men simply don't understand what's going on in women's heads. Sprinkle on a pregnancy, five thousand years of history and culture (still counting), a little superstition and a few taboos, and you can count us out completely. Not to make it any easier, I saw a Chinese health magazine with this mystifying English headline: "Chinese women have unique ambiguous implies". Women of the world and in this case specifically China, please know this: Trust me, we men are trying, we are really trying to understand the fairer sex, but it is a daunting task for us poor fellows. But what do you expect? We can't even master the art of multitasking! How on earth would we, the slow, insensitive, in theory a lean, mean, problem-solving machine, but in reality forever testosterone-controlled (read: out of control) cave men, ever learn to fathom the most complex beings on the face of this planet? And if you're one of those guys who just thought you had found the key to understanding 'the fairer sex', then you can think again if your wife has fallen pregnant. Nothing will ever be the same again.

2

I KISSED THE TEACHER

SINCE THIS BOOK is primarily about my wife Fu and me, let me give you a little introduction to the both of us and how we met.

Fu hails from the capital of spice in Southwest Central China, Chongqing, where she was born during the Cultural Revolution, just a few months after Richard Nixon's famous visit, which ended 25 years of no communication between the United States and China. Sitting in the confluence of the Yangtze and Jialing Rivers, 'The City of Fog', is a humongous sprawl of a city built in a mountainous area and nearly always covered in a thin mist. Along with Wuhan and Nanjing, it's one of the three 'furnace' cities (*san da huolu*) in the Yangtze River valley because of the especially hot and oppressively humid summer weather with temperatures often above 40 degrees for weeks.

Girls from Sichuan are known for the spicy food they eat and this is mirrored by a similarly fiery temperament, hence their nickname, *la meizi* meaning 'spice girls'. They are considered to be talkative, virtuous, openhearted, hardworking and tough with delicate and attractive skin (although pregnancy can alter this last attribute for a while). On top of this, girls from Chongqing and Chengdu often come in as number one or two on the "Top Ten Cities in China with the Most Beautiful Women"–hit list. Moreover, with a father-in-law from Chengdu and a mother-in-law from Chongqing, I should be home safe. Fu charmingly lives up to both nickname and reputation. A few lines from the popular Chinese song, *la meizi* by China's most famous soprano, Song Zuying, says it well: "She is hot, she is hot, yo. She speaks with passion, She moves with passion, She will welcome you warmly, Chilli gives the spice of life".

I'd say three Chinese characters can fully describe her: *Malatang* (I hope she will forgive me). Calm on the surface, but with all the tasty goodies bubbling just underneath, *malatang* is a famous street food from Chongqing and one of Fu's favourite dishes. It consists of skewered vegetables and meat cooked in a simmering scalding (*tang*) hot and spicy (*la*) chilli soup with pickled chilies, broad bean sauce, ginger and of course Sichuan pepper. Sichuan pepper or *huajiao* in Chinese, is actually not even a pepper, but little berries from a small shrub. It is gorgeous mildly hot and has a slightly lemony flavour which makes your tongue sing and dance and leaves you with a tingling numbness (*ma*) in the mouth–just like after a visit to the dentist, but in a good way.

One of her first, and not very flattering impression of foreigners in Mao's China in the mid-seventies, was from a Sichuanese children's rhyme starting with: "One, two, one, big nosed foreigners are unreasonable. Stepping on my foot, what can I say?" Apart from this, her view of foreigners was mostly formed through the movies she saw in school, where the Chinese hero always killed the evil Japanese villain.

She is a beautiful (with a looked-for so-called '*guazilian*' 'melon seed face'), open-minded and talented artist and designer. Despite her initial slightly negative impression of foreigners, she later spent five years studying art in Hamburg, Germany, and is an excellent teacher of the arts, and not least an exquisite cook. And here I can quickly kill off one Chinese pregnancy myth: according to Chinese folklore, spicy food makes mothers produce girls, but so far we only seem to be able to make boys. This of course could be due to my bad foreign influence, and all that Viking blood!

Indeed, I hail from the small Scandinavian country of Denmark, now famous for being the favourite "model country" of some American politicians, and the "birthplace" of the art of *'hygge'* (pronounced hue-gah), which means cosiness, and basically is all about just being, rather than having, and lighting a whole lot of candles. Its people have many times been named as the happiest people in the world. Personality-wise I'm usually a very calm and patient person and maybe that's why a friend of mine calls me Buddha. Or perhaps it's because of my nearly-bald head, square-shaped face (according to the Chinese my face is *'guozi'* shaped, like the character 国, meaning country or nation), and protruding stomach... The latter was initially a statement of solidarity with Fu, but has been slightly difficult to get rid of ever since. Fu often calls me Superman (lovingly most of the time), but not because of my sexual stamina or the fact that I wear my underpants over my trousers, because by "*man*" she means the Chinese word for "slow". A very good indication of our different temperaments...

I have had a love affair with China and practically everything Chinese since I was around eleven years old and learned to say *ni hao* and count to ten from the cute new girl in the class, who was as blond and Danish as can be, but who had lived in China for some years. Actually it probably even started much earlier. When I was only one day old and still at the maternity hospital, to the fright of my parents, a bat landed on my head. My course was set for life. I just didn't know it yet. In China, unlike in the West, bats are very auspicious creatures because the word for good fortune–*'fu'*–is a homophone for the word for bat. And later, after I found out that we had an old wooden box of antique china painted with drawings of exotic faraway lands, which my great grandfather had bought directly from the sailors in the docks of Copenhagen, hidden away in the basement, my course was set. Many years later, I found out that the beautiful Chinese characters on the bottom of it actually said "Made in Japan"; but by then it was too late).

I arrived in China, which at that time had almost become my *promised land*, on a cold and foggy winter day in early February of 1995, suffering from severe jetlag. Everything from the sky, to buildings, people's clothes and their faces, seemed to blend into a monotonous greyish haze. At the time, my main impression of China was still formed through seeing Bernardo Bertolucci's 1987 masterpiece, The Last Emperor, as a thirteen year old. Puyi, The Forbidden City and its stories made a lasting impact on me, and the palaces have remained my favourite place in China ever since.

My first impression of China in real life was, not surprisingly, utter disappointment. The first week in Chengdu was a culture shock, and I had sincere doubts about whether or not it had been the right decision to go. It was, after all, at first glance, a far cry from Puyi's Imperial China with its colourful palaces, exotic customs and splendid outfits.

In the fall of 1994, after serving my eight months in the Danish army, I had applied for half a year's study of Chinese language and culture at Sichuan University in Chengdu, at the time a city of 10 million people and the capital in the province known as a Land of plenty. I went to Chengdu on the recommendation of my private Chinese teacher, Ane (who had taught me a little pinyin-the official romanization system for Chinese in Mainland China-and simple conversation), to get away from the expat centres of Shanghai and Beijing, and because I had developed an interest in the ethnic minorities of southwest China.

Despite my first, slightly naïve, disappointment after arriving in China in early 1995, I quickly fell in love with the city's slow pace, its plentiful cosy tea houses and delicious spicy *mala* cuisine (although admittedly my tongue, taste buds, and stomach did have a few quarrels with it in the beginning). On one particularly bad day after eating an incredibly spicy Sichuan hotpot (including pig's intestines and brains, duck's blood, dark green seaweed, tofu skin, small bony catfish, and ox tripe among other common ingredients) the night before with a mixed group of cheerful Chinese and foreign friends, I can still remember vividly reading graffiti on our dormitory's toilet door: "hotpot ruined my life", and thinking how right the engraver had been. I was surprised, to say the least, when I later learned that chilli was used as a miraculous cure for both diarrhea and hemorrhoids in traditional Chinese Medicine.

Luckily, I eventually recovered and got so used to Sichuan cuisine, maybe even addicted, that now I can't live without it. There is an old Chinese saying that, "When you go to Beijing, you see how low in rank you are. When you travel to Guangzhou, you realize how little money you've got. But when you come to Chengdu, you find out how large your appetite is." That is what happened to me. All in all, it will probably be no surprise to anyone that I also fell in love with one of the local 'spice girls'.

Sitting in a classroom with a few other Westerners, but mostly Japanese and Korean students, in freezing sub-zero temperatures, often sitting on top of my hands to keep them just a little warm, it wasn't long before I realized it wasn't going to be easy learning Chinese in the classroom. In one of the first lessons, the teacher came in, covered the black board in Chinese characters and asked us to copy it. At the time, I had literally no idea where to start or finish. Frequently, seeing my dilemma, a Korean or Japanese girl would take pity on me, take my notebook, and just copy the whole thing for me. Very sweet as it was, I didn't learn much Chinese from that. Classes were in general the rather dull 'repeat-after-me' kind. Most teachers had no training in effective pedagogy, and the vocabulary taught–such as names of Chinese villains and heroes from the classic novel, *Outlaws of the Marsh*–was often useless out in the real world, shopping in the local market in the alley behind our dormitory, or going out for dinner in one of the local low-key restaurants where everybody spoke the local Sichuan dialect anyway, far removed from the standard Mandarin we were being taught. It took me a long time to figure out that the locals weren't angry or fighting when they continuously said "*sazi*" to me or each other, when it just meant "what?" It just sounded like that.

Unsurprisingly, after a month of diligent study, my mind started to wonder off, and I started to skip classes, looking for other more interesting ways to learn the language and culture. Thanks more or less to luck, I found several language conversation partners, some of them interesting and fun, others uptight and tight-lipped. With them, it was as if I had been assigned to a North Korean agent, and conversation quickly ran dry. Therefore, like many other of my friends in the dormitory, I went travelling, and once in a while I also went travelling with my language exchange partners.

One of the first things I had done after my arrival was to buy a huge map of China to hang over my bed. Now, more and more often, looking at it and trying to pronounce the many interesting-sounding names evoking thoughts of faraway mountain villages, untrodden paths, and wild and ethnic minorities with exotic names such as the Naxi, Mosuo, Lahu, Lisu, Miao, Dulong, Yi, Qiang, and Tibetans among many others, I took off on several backpacking adventures. As neither the teachers nor the university seemed to care if we attended classes or not, the travelling gradually took over and my Chinese language skills improved while on the road. However, Chengdu kept pulling me back and I ended up spending almost two years there.

While in Chengdu, where I gradually became a more diligent student, I also joined in the fun of doing movies and commercials in my spare time. Every other day, a Chinese movie scout or producer showed up in the dormitory, knocking on doors looking for a *laowai* (foreigner) fitting a specific and often rather obscure role or idea in his or her head. As long as we were foreign, talent was no concern. I acted in a TV series set in the 1880s, playing an evil French general armed to the teeth with a fake monocular telescope and plastic sword leading a battalion of vicious foreign devils, all my classmates from the dormitory. I also appeared in several very low-budget TV commercials, most of them rather surreal. One was for a Chinese anti-dementia medicine brand and featured an 80-something Chinese gentleman with a long white beard. He and I sat down to play chess together. That is, half the board was Western chess, and the other half was Chinese, an improbability of course, but just about when he was about to lose, he swallowed the wonder drug and then miraculously I was checkmated. Another commercial I did was together with a female classmate who was actually a former model. As the new fresh faces of the local beer brand, *Lanjian Pijiu* (Blue Sword Beer), we played along with the photographer's rather suggestive ideas of foreigners being very promiscuous, and poured several bottles of the rather flat and lukewarm 'Blue Sword' down each other's throats. Remarkably, it ran for two consecutive years on Chengdu TV, every night at 6.30 pm.

I also spent many weekends cycling around town on my

very own Flying Pigeon bicycle. First hand, day by day, I was witnessing the transformation of the city. I often got off the bike to talk to the locals about what was going on around them. On many occasions, I saw them packing up a whole life's worth of belongings onto the back of a tricycle, and the last thing many of them did was to take down the sign with the house number or even the street sign. Occasionally, I asked if I could have it as a souvenir, and most often, they said yes, even lending me the screwdriver to do the dismantling myself. I now have a whole collection of these old blue enamel signs at our place. I very much regretted seeing the city's old quarters torn down at such lightning speed, but I also feel thankful I got a chance to experience it before it was too late, as Chengdu is today unrecognizable to anyone who knew it as it had been for so many decades and even centuries. Gradually during that period, I also developed another hobby which has become a long-time fascination: visiting flea- and antique markets around town, admiring items and spending a little pocket money on Chinese curios and art.

One September day in 1997, contrary to some of the other foreign students who started kongfu, taichi or playing the *erhu* (the Chinese fiddle), I decided I wanted to learn the art of *shanshuihua*, literally, "mountain-water painting", more commonly known as Chinese "landscape painting". My kind Chinese teacher, Shi *laoshi* (teacher Shi), introduced me to an art teacher, fresh out of the Sichuan Institute of Fine Arts, the lovely and cool Deng Fu who, while smoking Zhongnanhai cigarettes that used to be specially made for Chairman Mao (even though he seems to have preferred other brands), but had become very popular among young smokers in China, accepted the challenge of teaching a hopeless foreign student. I studied it with passion and vigour for the first few months and we became good friends.

However when talent and concentration couldn't be stretched much further, we often ended up touring flea markets, local sights, narrow streets, and small restaurants where Fu introduced me to the joys of eating spicy rabbit heads, among other local delicacies. And of course the tea houses and bamboo parks, for which Chengdu is famous, full of people lounging around on bamboo chairs nearly all hours of the day and the dark bamboo groves full of lustful university students at night. My conclusion based upon all my experiences in Chengdu, the cosy afternoons sipping green tea with Fu, and the raucous parties in the foreign students' building, was that, as the Chinese philosopher Lin Yutang said it, "Tea is invented for quiet company as wine is invented for a noisy party".

Five years later, after finishing my master's degree in Chinese and East Asian studies with a thesis initially based on a project for the United Nations Office on Drugs and Crime, on opium usage and the anti-opium campaigns in the minority and frontier regions of southwest China, I relocated to Beijing. Here, after a few stints of living in plain and boring apartments in concrete blocks, I moved into a newly rebuilt two storey neotraditional Beijing courtyard house, called a *siheyuan*, a stone's throw east of the Forbidden City and a ten-minute walk away from Tiananmen Square. Now I could finally gaze on its golden-glazed tiled roofs and massive crimson walls whenever I opened my front door. The first bright and clear morning, on which I saw the rising sun reflecting off those golden rooftops, while hearing all the unfamiliar street sounds coming from the grinder, the barber, the lady collecting bottles, another one selling sesame candy, a third selling freshly-cut lamb, and all the other local peddlers walking or bicycling through our street, each with their individual call, I felt like a thirteen-year-old again. At that moment, looking

I KISSED THE TEACHER

towards that fabled palace that I had dreamt of visiting so many times as a teenager, I felt right at home.

The area I had moved to was originally a part of the Imperial City itself, enclosed by high crimson walls and a canal, and it stored supplies like porcelain, silk, meat, lanterns and grain for the emperor's household. It had been off limits to the general public until the last dynasty, the Qing, succumbed in 1911. But in the years following it had gradually become a popular area for foreigners to live in, and, as I found out, the Danish Embassy had even occupied a large and beautiful old courtyard in the area which was still there. Nanchizi Street which lay on the west side of my neighborhood, right along the Forbidden City's moat, with its grey brick one storey houses with small shops and restaurants shaded below the age old scholar trees, was one of only a handful left of traditional *hutong* (alley) with a perfectly preserved atmosphere of old Beijing. Its special history was still visible in many of the lane names in the area, such as the Porcelain Storeroom (*Ciqiku*) and the Lantern Storeroom (*Denglongku*) Hutong. Whenever workers were digging in Ciqiku Hutong, just 50 meters south of my courtyard the whole neighborhood came alive, buzzing with excitement as pieces of imperial porcelain started to reappear out of the ground. Just outside my front door towered the massive walls of the impressive Pudu-or Mahakala Temple, dating back to the fifteenth century, when it had been the prison of an exposed Ming emperor before he once again was able to usurp the throne. Later on it was the home of the Manchu prince, Dorgon, whose troops had conquered Beijing in 1644 unopposed and who effectively became the ruler during the early Manchu occupation of China. Dorgon also introduced the policy of forcing all Han Chinese men to shave the front of the heads and wear their hair in queues just like the Manchus. When he died in a hunting accident, the buildings were converted into a Buddhist Mongolian Lama temple. The foreigners who leased courtyards here in the 1930s, told stories of waking up to the sound of the monks chanting. Before it was renovated around 2003, for the past several decades, it had idled away a life as a local primary school. Both the monks and the little kids were gone now, but a few of the buildings and much of the atmosphere was still intact as the grounds were converted to a park and the buildings served as the new, and, as the name suggests, not very sexy, Beijing Taxation Museum. I spent many hours in the old temple grounds watching locals do taichi, kicking a *jianzi* (shuttlecock) around with friends or reading underneath the gingko trees. In the fall, golden leaves turned the temple's ground into a yellow ocean. My small two-storey, south-facing house was almost brand new and made of concrete instead of the traditional wood beam construction. Although lacking in traditional charm, it was actually really cosy, and contrary to most traditional courtyards, also had its own toilet and bathroom, as well as a closed circuit central heating system, which, as winter temperatures and Siberian winds set in, even made the birds outside happy. The area around Pudu Temple was mainly inhabited by local Beijingers who had lived their whole life in the area, sprinkled on with a few Chinese millionaires whom we rarely saw outside of their black-tinted luxury cars, but who owned huge courtyards around the block, and a little foreign community. I shared the courtyard with three other families: The Li's, a traditional and very friendly, three generations under one roof Beijing family, their Cocker Spaniel, Lucky which sadly was lame on its hind legs, and their only child, shy, high school kid *Daren* as the youngest branch on the Li family tree and on whom they placed the whole family's future aspirations and hopes. My landlords' parents, the Hao's, a retired and quiet cook with the People's Liberation Army, who had served in Malta and his cheerful and chatty wife, who often showed up in my living room when I least expected it, both in their late seventies. And last but not least, another Danish couple, my friends taichi-master Nils and IT specialist Marie, who recommended the house to me. They also introduced me to their favorite hole in the wall Xinjiang restaurant around the corner with great service, beautiful lamb and chicken heart skewers accompanied by ice-cold Yanjing draft beer. However before the 2008 Olympics, the whole area of remaining *hutong* and courtyards including the small restaurant between our courtyard and Beijing's main shopping street, Wangfujing, was torn down in the so-called beutification campaign to give way to more shining shopping malls and fancy restaurants.

A few more years passed, and that's when it happened. One day, nearly ten years after Fu and I first met, I kissed the teacher, and not long after, she moved into the courtyard in Pudu Temple East Lane No. 2 with me.

3

WHAT DOES SHE WANT?

IN THE 1970s, public displays of affection, not to mention marrying a foreigner, were not only inconceivable, but also close to impossible, and there were officially no interracial marriages registered in mainland China. In 1978, when a Liaoning university graduate and a French female student applied for marriage, the local government had to report to the Ministry of Civil Affairs for approval because it could not find a legal basis. In fact, government figures on the number of Chinese-foreign marriages registered in China only became available in 1979, when China started opening up to the world. In 1979, less than 300 out of 8,500 couples who registered a Chinese-foreign marriage in mainland China were with foreigners from outside Hong Kong, Macau, and Taiwan. Since then, tens of thousands of Chinese have married foreigners each year, and in 2001, that number had reached 26,000 out of 79,000 in total. Until the early 1990s, Chinese marrying foreigners was still an unusual event in mainland China. Specific numbers for the whole of China, however, are hard to come by, but a Chinese article online from 2015 entitled "Which nationality does Chinese girls love to marry?", says said that figure decreased to just over 47,000 couples in 2014. These numbers are also very unevenly spread across China's vast territory. According to a Chinese article in

WHAT DOES SHE WANT?

Renkou yu Jingji (Population and Economics) in 2013, on A Study on Cross-Nation Marriage of Beijing, it is clear that the majority of marriages to foreigners was in the Northeast and, most prevalent, in the South-eastern coastal provinces. In Guangdong alone, nearly 370,000 were married to foreigners between 1979 and 2010. Only in 2010, did Beijing come in to fifth place, and at its peak, the number of foreign marriage registrations between the Beijing Olympics and 2012, was 5507, but fell afterwards to 4750 in the next four-year period. However, the number of Chinese women marrying foreign men has always been several times greater than the other way around. Take Beijing as an example from a 2019 Chinese article. Yang Kaiheng writes that among the more than 18,700 foreign-related marriages registered from 1998 to 2017, Chinese women marrying foreign men accounted for 73%. In some areas the percentage has been as high as nearly 90%. Although it seems though the *laowai* are losing their charm, as the overall numbers have dropped, the number of interracial marriages between Chinese and Africans are on the rise as a direct result from China's increasing investment in, and trade with, Africa.

Like anywhere else around the world, it's not always easy to be a foreigner dating a local. A widely circulated, commented and reposted article by a female Chinese writer has been translated on a favourite website of mine, *Chinasmack.com*, as: "Chinese women! Please don't sleep with foreigners", and it started out by stating that: "Ask a foreigner why he has come to China. He'll probably answer that he likes China's long history, splendid culture, rapid development and changes." However, she went on to state that, "the overwhelming majority are here for two reasons: The first, they can't support themselves very well at home, or maybe even can't support themselves at all. The second, for Chinese girls!"

After that, I hardly dare to say that I am actually very interested in China's long history…

A Weibo user named "Dr. Xie 88" stated in his post that it is appalling that men outnumber women by 33 million in China, and bombastically commented:

"Considering there are millions of Chinese men who can't find a spouse, if the authorities continue to introduce large numbers of foreign students into the country or advocate interracial marriages between Chinese women and foreign men, this will be a crime against the Chinese race. They will leave behind a historical monument of shame."

The Larry King of China, the host of China Central Television's (CCTV) daily English talk show, *Dialogue*, a man called Yang Rui, also joined in the bashing. In 2012, he said on Weibo: "Behead the snake heads [human traffickers], the unemployed Americans and Europeans who come to China to make money, trafficking in people, misleading the public and encouraging them to emigrate," he started out. "Identify the foreign spies, who find a Chinese woman to cohabit with, while their job is to collect intelligence, drawing maps and perfecting GPS." It needs mention that Yang Rui drew heavy criticism in particular for his anti-foreign remarks and even state media *Global Times* condemned his insensitive comments.

I don't dare to mention that during my years in Beijing, I did in fact work on both the collecting and selling of Chinese maps, and historical maps of China and its cities on a regular basis.

However, it seems as though Yang Rui might actually be onto something. While walking down a *hutong* just north of the Art Museum in central Beijing, I noticed two posters on a wall. It was a vivid comic book story of how a foreigner called Dawei (David) coerces the innocent Miss Li, who has fallen in love with him, to revealing state secrets. It turns out, the police tell her, that he is in fact a spy and she risks up to ten years in prison. After I posted pictures of these public notices on my Facebook account, a Chinese friend of mine commented: "There are 50,000 foreign spies living in Beijing, Hong Kong, Urümqi and Shanghai".

Luckily, I have never sensed any of these prejudices in my in-laws. My father-in-law is a very upright, talkative, retired factory manager, head of the propaganda department and Communist Party boss, formerly one of the top leaders of Chongqing Iron and Steel factory with more than 80,000 workers, who admirably continuously turned down bribes and every other day returned "gifts" to the factory offices. Many of his former colleagues ended up spending years in prison on charges of corruption. My sweet and quiet mother-in-law used to work in one of the factory's laboratories as a chemist and after retiring, she worked ten more years as an accountant. My first gifts to them were rather disastrous. I presented my father-in-law with a bottle of whisky, but, as mentioned earlier, he usually doesn't, and actually can't, drink alcohol. And despite all the books I had read on Chinese cultural habits which all specifically point out that you do not give a Chinese person anything sharp or pointy as a gift, because it insinuates that you want to cut off your relationship with them, I gave my mother-in-law a porcelain kitchen knife. Since then, not surprisingly, I have never seen it.

Although we have had differences of opinion, of course, and they have had (and still have) many questions, we have always had a good relationship. There was one question, however, that luckily they did not have to ask. My father-in-law told me that when he was a little boy in Chengdu, a few years before the Communist liberation at a time when foreigners were being asked to leave China, there was a small church next door where a foreign missionary lived with his family. My father-in-law and his two friends had been told that foreigners had tails like monkeys, so after observing some of them from a safe distance sitting in a tall tree, they decided to climb over the fence to see if it was true. A little blond boy was out playing, and while the other two boys where making funny faces, my father-in-law snuck up behind the unwitting boy and stuck his hand down the back of his pants. To his surprise, he found no tail. The little foreigner was of course startled and started crying for his mommy and the three Chinese boys ran out of the courtyard as fast as they could. I am just happy that my father-in-law had already cleared this up before I married his daughter.

Meanwhile many foreigners, men as well as women, think that foreign men dating and marrying Chinese women are only doing so for two reasons: because they can't find a girlfriend in their own country, and because they want to have a beautiful, docile wife who does the housework while smiling quietly. Maybe some foreigners still believe China is stuck in imperial times where a man could have several wives, the women walked around on three-inch lily feet, and a husband could terminate the marriage for reasons such as neglect of his parents, wanton conduct, jealousy and loquacity. Just to be clear: That is not the case!

Western stereotypes of Chinese women often portray them as soft, delicate, shy, alluring, and almost elf-like. This is, unsurprisingly, not in any way reflective of real life. Although actually, the alluring bit is true. Personally, I feel it has generally become a lot easier to go out in public as a mixed couple, especially compared to when I first came to China twenty five years ago. Stares are a lot less common these days. Nonetheless, glares still do sometimes get hurled, and I sometimes catch myself returning them with vengeful wrath! And the glares certainly haven't diminished since having children. As a family,

WHAT DOES SHE WANT?

we have been the cause of numerous close-call traffic incidents with people literally walking into trees or street lights and ending up millimetres from being run over just because they were busy scrutinizing our children or looking up at us. Prejudice is difficult to get rid of, and that goes both ways. The stereotypical scenario among Chinese is that Chinese girls who marry foreign guys always marry balding old farts, the same age as their own fathers, and they do it for the foreign passport and/or the money. Admittedly, I have seen a few examples of this, but it is far from being always the case. Furthermore, this trend of beautiful young girls marrying rich old guys seems to be quite normal among Chinese nationals themselves. There is even a very popular school in Beijing called The Moral Education School for Girls which is full of Chinese women dreaming of marrying a rich Chinese man and thus studying the skills (including how to be charming, apply pretty make-up, and pour a perfect cup of tea) apparently needed to be able to eventually fulfil this dream. As part of chasing this dream, Chinese dating shows are on every channel almost every night.

One Sunday night we were again watching the hugely popular Chinese dating show "If You Are the One" on television and suddenly, out of the blue, my bachelor friend Kasper who owns a company designing and selling women's shoes, appeared on screen. In front of 24 Chinese prospective female dates and about 50 million Chinese viewers (and potential customers), he presented himself as the perfect catch. The main explanation for its popularity lies in the bachelorettes often very direct questions, which frequently focus on "grilling" the man about his financial situation, the size of his house and bank account, and which car he drives. In one of the show's first episodes, a female participant famously remarked that she would "prefer to cry in a BMW" than laugh riding on the back of a bicycle. The focus on wealth and so-called gold-diggers made the Communist Party and their censors nervous and so they threatened to shut down the programme for "showcasing and hyping up money-worship". So, with a few changes, the show has been running for ten years now and is attracting millions of viewers both in China and abroad.

In the end, Kasper did indeed leave the show with his beautiful and charming "heartbeat girl" (*xindong nüsheng*), although, for the record, after a few dates it apparently wasn't *the one*.

It also seems to be a 'truth' among Chinese in general that the Chinese girls who marry foreigners are not beautiful, in the classic Chinese sense of the word, anyway. Now, as you know, beauty is in the eye of the beholder. For instance, no Chinese I know thinks the American-born Chinese Hollywood actress, Lucy Liu is beautiful; for god's sake, she has freckles! Many Westerners would certainly say otherwise. Apparently, even Chinese movie star Zhang Ziyi, who has been voted as one of the world's most beautiful women by *People* Magazine, is considered only "so-so" by many Chinese, and there was once even a blog on the *China Daily* website entirely devoted to the question: "Do Foreign Men Have Ugly Chinese Girlfriends?" My question, then, is this: What's all the fuss about, if we foreign men are only taking the "ugly" left over women?

As it happens, in China, the rather sexist and derogatory term "leftover woman," *sheng nu*, has become widely used to describe an urban, well-educated, often wealthy, professional female over the age of 27 who is still single. There might be more than 500,000 *sheng nu* in Beijing alone! It is no secret that China's One Child Policy, now abandoned but probably too late, has resulted in a surplus of up to 30 million men who will not be able to find a bride. A fact that would logically lead to the conclusion that the marriage market is skewed heavily in favour of girls. However, the Chinese government has for years spun a massive media campaign, which basically, conveys the message to women that: "If you want to stand a snowball's chance in hell of ever getting married in this country, don't demand too much from your man."

It is a deep-rooted belief in China that a woman must marry up in social class (known as hypergamy), meaning that the norm in a relationship is that males are expected to be higher in every sense, including height, age, education and salary. This was made very clear when, in 2010, the website of the state's supposedly feminist All-China Women's Federation carried out a nationwide survey in which "More than 90 percent of men surveyed said women should marry before 27 to avoid becoming unwanted." In the end, they had to delete the articles about leftover women because so many Chinese women complained. This rather sexist, albeit humorous, little song has circulated on the Chinese internet, and it clearly conveys the popular sentiment that women's desirability declines with age.

"A 20-year old woman is like a basketball,
Everyone is scrambling for it.
A 30-year old woman is like a ping pong ball,
Everyone is hitting it back and forth.
A 40-year old woman is like a soccer ball,
Everyone wants to kick it.
A 50-year old woman is like a golf ball,
The further away it is hit, the better."

All in all, this leads to a phenomenon in which A-grade men marry B-grade women, B-grade men marry C-grade women and so on. The only ones left are A-grade women and D-grade men. This skewed imbalance has even led to a niche market opportunity. A Shanghai business woman, Liang Yali, has had great success with her "Seek-a-Husband" course, which specializes in teaching Chinese women (mainly A-grade women, *sheng nu* above 35) how to find and marry a *laowai* knight-in-shining-armor (perhaps even "handsome like a Nazi" as my young female Chinese colleague blurted out when 6' 2" Florian from our German office was visiting. Luckily he did not hear it…). I found an article on a Chinese match-making company website, which even listed six advantages of marrying a foreigner. First of all, foreigners are romantic. They say "I love you" all the time. Secondly, they are all handymen and can fix things such as the toilet, the car, the door etc. Thirdly, life is simple with a foreigner. You can scold all you want, as long as it is in Chinese, he won't understand it. Fourthly, foreigners can't see the difference between an ugly girl and a pretty girl, a country girl or even an older leftover woman. As long as you have long hair and red lips, and you can cook him a simple bowl of noodles he is happy. Fifthly, the whole world (read: all of China) will be jealous of you when you give birth to handsome mixed blood (*hunxue*) children. And lastly, it is a fashion among foreign men to marry a Chinese woman. A very interesting list of "facts" indeed. And maybe partly as a result of this, China now "exports" up to four times more women than it "imports"! I am just happy I got an A!

In my (and to many others) opinion, Fu still looks like she could be 29. I, on the other hand, probably look somewhat older than my real age, especially to most Chinese, because of my balding head, protruding stomach, and beard, which at a point also reached nearly Taliban-like proportions, causing Chinese to, more and more often, nervously ask Fu about my origins. So not unsurprisingly, most people in our neighbourhood believed me to be ten or more years her senior, even though she is actually two years older than me.

We were at a friend's birthday party one hot and humid

WHAT DOES SHE WANT?

evening in June, of course indulging in yet another meal of Sichuan hotpot, and across from Fu and I sat a Chinese artist, his wife and a Chinese friend. Their friend had been staring at us for some time and then leaned over and asked the artist while looking in the direction of Fu: "What does she see in that foreign old fart?"

Fu heard him, I didn't. She told me only later, as she didn't want to ruin the birthday party.

As mentioned before, I can't deny that I have seen such cases of 'foreign old farts with young Chinese wives, but they no longer account for the majority of "mixed couples". The average age difference between a Chinese bride and her foreign husband was over 10 years, but the official statistics say that has now changed. Nevertheless, one day when I was taking a stroll with a friend in our neighbourhood, we were talking about some of my funny experiences and the prejudice against mixed couples, and I looked at all the mixed couples passing by. We met four couples in ten minutes within just 400 metres of each other. Surprisingly, without exception, they were all in this category, with an age difference of around 15-30 years, plus a toddler in a stroller. And I had just been telling my friend that it was not that common anymore to see such mixed couples …

Luckily trends and attitudes are changing, but still expect to get the third degree anywhere you go in China, but then that applies to pretty much all people with foreign-looking faces not just people in mixed race relationships! I am usually fine with the normal chit-chat and unavoidable questions concerning life, income and other things you would usually only consider raising with very close friends, if at all. But that's not the case in China.

One pleasant spring afternoon, we were at the playground in a park in Beijing, when Fu got yet another full interrogation by a middle-aged woman with bobbed hair dyed reddish sitting next to her on the bench. "Where are you from? Where is he from? Have you ever been there? What do you do and what does he do? What does his parents do? How much did their house and car cost? How much do you earn, and how much does he earn? Where do you live? How much is the rent? Do you take care of the baby alone or do you have an *ayi* (nanny)? How much does she cost? How old are you and how old is he? He looks like a good man and father, is he?.... The questions kept coming like machine-gun fire. She was on an unstoppable roll. Fu was close to saying, "No, he beats both me and the children all the time," just to stop the woman, but finally the questions dried up, just short of, "So what was the conception like?"

To be fair, age can be equally difficult to tell for Chinese and Westerners alike. I received a serious blow below the belt one day when yet another middle-aged Chinese lady asked me if I was the grandfather. Maybe it's time to lose the beard that I've had since I played that evil French general in a Chinese TV series in my university days in Chengdu; or maybe I should try and contact Elton John or Wayne Rooney and get some tips on hair transplants. On the other hand, I once asked a new part-time colleague at work if she was still in high school. She turned out to be 28 years old!

4

IF I HAD A MILLION DOLLARS

WE WERE ALREADY too late. We found out that anyone who gets pregnant in Beijing will generally book a place at one of the big maternity hospitals before the sixth week into their pregnancy. If you come later than this, you have to know someone on the inside–*zhao guanxi* – or you can forget all about it. Alternatively, it would have to be a small local hospital, a public VIP ward, or otherwise the only option left would be private.

We have two Chinese friends who got married, and even before the wife has any idea of whether or not she can even get pregnant, her main concern is which hospital to go to for the check-ups and delivery. The happy couple have already visited several hospitals, and while it is understandable that when you are only allowed one child, as was the case at the time, you want everything to be perfect. I do think that the guy was secretly looking forward to at least a few months of early marriage bliss before starting to think about familial expansion.

After working in Chengdu for a few months, Fu came back to Beijing, carrying all the necessary papers from the local authorities, approving her pregnancy and allowing her to deliver the one child she was then entitled to under the family planning system of the People's Republic. She was however already four months pregnant upon her return so options for us to choose a hospital to actually deliver this little wonder boy (the gender of which we of course did not yet know at this point in time) were indeed very limited. First, we started out by looking at the major public maternity hospitals, but quickly realized that it would be nigh on impossible to get in, even through a connection. The only replies we got were "No", "No", and, "You can forget about it–you are way too late!" So what to do? As we did not feel comfortable choosing one of the lesser known local options, fearing both lack of expertise and sanitary standards, we began looking further afield. One alternative we considered was for Fu to go and stay with her parents in Chengdu where both checkups and the delivery itself would have been paid for in part by her work unit (*danwei*). Health insurance in China unfortunately still follows the *danwei* and *hukou*-system, so even though in theory it would be possible to be reimbursed for invoices from a Beijing-based hospital, in practise it would be so complicated and Time-consuming (travelling back and forth to Chengdu for the right stamps), that it would not really count as an option. Nevertheless, since I wouldn't have been able to attend many of the check-ups, scans and ultrasounds, and could have missed the delivery altogether if she was to have stayed in Chengdu, we decided to continue our search for a local Beijing option.

Anyway, how could I expect my pregnant wife to get up in the morning at 3-4 am to go and stand in line in front of the local obstetrics hospital? Or even go there at 6 am to buy a number from one of the many number touts/scoundrels who make money by selling numbers to stand in line? Even when you do get a number, you can expect to spend the major part of the day at the hospital waiting your turn. In the end, we did get into one of Beijing's reputable public hospitals with a so-called '*guibin lou*' (VIP ward), through a *guanxi* there, but after a few visits we had to admit to ourselves, that even though the

IF I HAD A MILLION DOLLARS

doctor finished the examination in less than three minutes every time and said everything was okay, we were kind of wondering if she was doing all the necessary tests, or if perhaps she was expecting something more from us? When time after time we saw other people giving expensive perfume, beauty cream, and French wine, indiscreetly placed on the doctor's desk, we kind of got the idea.... If you have been in China for a while, this is not surprising, but still.

We decided to go for a private hospital instead. And oh my, are they expensive. Prices at private hospitals are pretty much like prices in private hospitals in the US if you don't have insurance. At the time, a normal delivery including a prenatal and postpartum package, would easily relieve your wallet of about RMB 80,000-100,000 (roughly US$13-16,000 at the time). And prices go up every year. Some friends of ours, an American-Chinese couple, were looking to spend north of RMB 150,000 for their upcoming delivery at a local private hospital, and the main reason behind this expensive choice was because his American mother thought it was the only viable and safe local option–so she paid. In any case, expectant parents here might as well get used to it. I read in the *New York Times* that the costs of having a baby and raising it to the age of eighteen, everything included, would come to around US$2 million! This amount is actually a conservative estimate and in most cases would certainly not be enough for Beijing. With costs of a kindergarten in Beijing at the time often exceeding RMB 80,000 to 120,000 a year, and sometimes higher, and when the costs of even a cheap international school will easily set you back double or even triple that amount, then US$2 million would not be near enough. Far from it.

Luckily, for the birth, we found a slightly cheaper private option, where the price difference from the public VIP ward was actually not that big. And one of the disadvantages of public

Chinese hospitals, anyway, is that the father cannot be present at the delivery, neither at the normal ward nor at the VIP ward.

In any case, giving birth in a private maternity hospital in China is like staying in a five-star hotel for four days (probably with a little more pain though), and who wouldn't want that? In Denmark you would normally be in and out of the hospital on the same day. You are sent home just about as soon as the doctor has cut the umbilical cord, or I am sure it feels like that to most new parents at least when driving home or sat on a public bus just two or three hours after giving birth, completely clueless as to what awaits them.

Or we could also simply leave it to fate as our good friends had (inadvertently) done by delivering out in the open. An American mother and Chinese-Australian father, who were having their third baby, had decided that when contractions started they could walk to the hospital, but what should have been a 15-minute stroll at 4 am, turned into a healthy baby girl born on the street just a few metres before the hospital entrance about half an hour later. The proud father said afterwards that it reminded him of his rugby days, "It was like trying to catch a 3.7kg buttered water balloon".

Luckily, three 'wise men' came in the form of local drunks, on their way home from *zhapi* and *yangrouchuan'r*-large mugs of local beers and grilled lamb skewers. They had clearly had a few too many ("*guanle maoniao*", literally "guzzled cat piss", as the Chinese would sometimes say), and were wearing sleeveless vests, of the type called 'wife-beaters' in the West (worthy of Onslow from Keeping Up Appearances). Actually, in China these garments are known as *bang ye* ("shoulder grandpa"), or just simply *baolukuang* ("exhibitionist"). The Beijing authorities almost begged local men to stop wearing them during the Olympics for fear of *losing* face and being deemed uncivilized by the many visiting foreign spectators. Especially because of the comfortable but not so aesthetic (six-packs are not prevalent, think more "Buddha belly") Chinese habit of rolling them up to uncover their bellies as a means of cooling down in the hot and humid summers. Actually it has become popular among expats to call this style the "Beijing bra"!

No doubt, these men couldn't believe their own eyes, or perhaps the amount of alcohol they had consumed, when they saw a foreign woman giving birth on the street and her husband holding the baby in his arms with the umbilical cord still attached. Fortunately they sobered up quickly enough and ran for help at the hospital. Even though it was surely a dramatic experience for all involved, everything went well, all were fine, and the mother didn't even miss a meal. What perfect timing!

With the hospital finally settled on, Fu and I were ready for everything that would come our way, or at least that's what I thought.

5

I COULDN'T HELP BUT NOTICE

A WELL-DRESSED, beautiful woman walking by a group of men would, at the very least, not go unnoticed where I'm from. I have to admit that if a gorgeous member of the opposite sex walks past me, I might well start staring in spite of myself. Not so the Chinese male. If you have been to China, you might have noticed how subtle Chinese men can be when it comes to not looking up or even noticing when a stunning beauty walks past them. Or so it seems. Maybe it is good manners or shyness. But a lady from Spain who had spent half a year in Beijing once asked me, "How can they not look?" She simply had no idea how Chinese men seemed to not notice or pay attention to the stunning local women walking past them. How do they do it? Do they really not look, even peek just a little? Her coming from Spain, where something like this would not happen in a million years, if ever (her words not mine), I could see her point. I told her I was sure that they did indeed look. But how do they do it so elegantly and discreetly?

Fu explained to me how culture and tradition in China teaches boys not to look or stare openly at a woman, and they would be deemed unmannered and uncultured if they did so, and somewhat of a *liumang*-meaning something pervert-if they ever thought of calling out something like "*Ciao bella!*" or "*Hola *guapa!*". Lately, however, it has actually become quite common to hear the expressions "*meinü*" (beautiful woman) and "*shuaige*" (handsome guy), just like the equivalent of the British "Love", or the American "darling", whenever you enter a cafe or a small shop.

In China, it all boils down to "face", whether face is gained or lost. The Chinese concept of face can be difficult for a foreigner to grasp. The famous Chinese writer and translator Lin Yutang, who tried to define Chinese-ness in his best-selling book *My Country and My People* in the 1930s, gave up and said that, "Face cannot be translated or defined." He did, however, characterize it thus: "Abstract and intangible, it is yet the most delicate standard by which Chinese social intercourse is regulated."

Maybe the closest English translations would be something like "honour", "pride", "dignity" or "prestige". However you translate it, it is all about how one is viewed by others, or how you view yourself as being viewed. "Face" can also be both given and earned, as well as taken away or lost. For thousands of years, Chinese culture has been putting emphasis on the family, clan or group over the individual. Face can be lost for behaviour deemed by society to be immoral or socially disagreeable. Face is a sociological thing, not a psychological thing, meaning that it doesn't exist in a person, but is distributed 'out there' in society.

It is fair to say one is not born with the notion of face, so it must get "inserted" somehow. I have always wondered and been fascinated by how "face" becomes a part of a Chinese person's life–how does it get under their skin, so to speak? Is it social inheritance, through the genes, or possibly even the food–or maybe a combination?

Actually, I have a personal theory of how face is learned. No, not through breast feeding; I think Chinese people get it in a kind of cultural 'two for the price of one' package.

Here is an example of how 'face' works in action. A commonly-seen scenario on Chinese streets could look like this: Driver of vehicle A, a black Audi A6 with tinted windows, is an inch away from crashing into vehicle B, a city bus with 148 people pressed up against the windows and seemingly unconcerned by what is going on outside although that could be due to a lack of oxygen. The bus is also surrounded by slow-moving motorbikes, bicycles and pedestrians–all at the bottom of the Chinese traffic food chain. Will you detect a glimmer of panic, fear or even the twitch of an eye on driver A's face? No! On the contrary, he or she will continue to stare the so-called thousand-yard stare (usually used to describe the blank, unfocused gaze of a battle-weary soldier) into the middle distance, with a face like chiselled marble, until the problem resolves itself. In this way, the driver has shown no face, and neither lost nor gained face. The driver has remained pretty much what you could call "face-less". I do, however, still think Driver A has surely registered every precarious second, well, at least the bus, and maybe even noticed at least one cyclist or a pedestrian (although I am unsure about this last bit).

But what about the "face" of pretty girls? All the young innocent Chinese women wearing outfits that, if worn in the West would be undeniably considered 'slutty', are somehow viewed in China much more innocently. Thus it's not uncommon to see girls on the streets dressed provocatively. But I must admit that one of the great things about living in China is the incredible contrasts that one sees and experiences every day. And I still can't help to be amazed and delighted when at 7 am, a young Chinese woman emerges from her home in one of Beijing's dilapidated alleyways looking like a million renminbi, hotter than Georgia asphalt, like she is going to the coolest night club in town or to an audition for the Chinese version of Dancing with the Stars. But probably she is on her way to the office, or maybe even the vegetable market. It's quite wonderful.

And it often makes me feel under-dressed, although fortunately Chinese men, particularly in Beijing, are usually almost as casually dressed as Scandinavian men. Fundamentally, it's about cultural interpretation, I guess. Chinese girls are no doubt taught that it is not refined to dress up in skimpy clothes and heels hardly made for walking. Nevertheless, a quick glance along the streets of any Chinese city will indicate that a generation of Chinese parents and schoolteachers have utterly failed. One could rightfully argue here that young women are simply desperate to dress up after twelve years of wearing the same shapeless sports pants and tops that make up China's androgynous school uniforms. Or maybe the concept of "face" is on its way out with much of the younger generation. I don't know. What I do know is that 'face' is very difficult to define and the concept itself is fluid and ever-changing.

That said, none of these cultural limitations and concepts of "face" hold the local men back when it comes to looking at foreign women. I have a Danish friend, an elegant, beautiful woman in her early fifties who gets hit on by drivers every time she gets in to a Beijing taxi. And they do not hide their intentions in any way, she tells me. The explanation here must be that somehow the "face" thing only really applies within the Chinese cultural sphere, and as such, the taxi drivers face no risk of losing face when approaching a foreign woman.

And when you have just gotten used to this, then everything will be turned on its head. With a pregnant wife, everybody stares–women as well as men. And allow me to let you in on a little secret: stare is not all they do...

You know you're going to be a dad in China when...?
Many of my friends who have become fathers in China were

eager to finish the sentence when I put it to them, so here are a few of my favorites.

"...your walls are suddenly plastered with posters of cute babies and toddlers"

"...your wife craves swallow's nest soup, chicken feet, ox tripe or stinky tofu at all times, 24/7"

"... your wife wants your mother to move in with you–and upon realizing that it is not going to happen, invites her mother to move in"

"... her family starts arguing over the name of the child"

".... waiting lists for a *peiyue* or *yuesao* (full-time nanny for the first month) come up regularly during dinner"

"...a fresh pack of reindeer antlers arrives from *Dongbei* [Northeast China]"

"... you haven't had sex for the last nine months"

I should save the last words for my British friend, Paul, who is married to a Shanghainese and whose humour is as dry as the Sahara. Here is what he said when I asked if he had a good story to tell about becoming a father. "My wife had taken UK citizenship by that time and we got on British Airways and went home for a year so I'm afraid ours was a perfectly normal UK NHS [National Health Service] experience with nothing Chinese about it at all. I did not marry a woman who did teddy bears or superstition and I made sure both her parents were dead so they couldn't interfere and I would never have let her near either a local hospital or doctor… I really don't have any Chinese stories about it at all–sorry."

6

TEACH ME TIGER

IN CHINA, it is generally believed that announcing a pregnancy within the first trimester will cause the pregnant woman to miscarry, so your wife may not have even told you yet. But there is one way you can know for sure. If you come home one day and find your lovely wife has cut her beautiful long black hair short, is without any make-up whatsoever, wearing oversized fluffy pink slippers, and is dressed in something that looks like a lead-lined-apron stolen from a nearby hospital X-ray room, or oversized overalls with a big cuddly teddy bear on the belly (worst case scenario: she is wearing both), you can be sure of what has happened: your partner is pregnant and is ready to tell the world. Talk about a makeover!

When we found out that Fu was pregnant (and I thank God it didn't happen the way I just described), we were, of course, very happy and thrilled that we were going to be parents, but quite soon afterwards, some rather unexpected surprises turned up– especially for me. Chinese folk beliefs surrounding a pregnant woman and how she should behave in order to protect the fetus are numerous, to say the least, and the validity of these beliefs is not open to debate. And it seems the whole world has an opinion.

Fu's sister in-law, Haihai was the first to join in the game enthusiastically and she was very much an 'expert'. Fu was duly instructed to no longer participate in weddings or funerals because she should avoid getting too excited, too sad or in any other way too emotional, as this could have a negative influence on the development of the fetus. In addition, she should under no circumstances go and visit her best friends who had just become parents to a baby boy. Newborn babies apparently possess a very strong *yang* energy which can harm an unborn child.

Haihai explained: "The god of unborn children, *Taishen*, can both protect and harm the fetus. *Taishen* always follows pregnant women around so you must constantly be careful not to insult him."

There was more. Moving the furniture around was off-limits, especially not in the bedroom, and she should not sew, knit, use scissors, or do anything that involved drilling, chopping, sawing or hammering in order to not insult Taishen, and to ensure that Fu would get enough rest to assist the fetus to grow.

"Otherwise you could give him a reason to harm the fetus, and even miscarry," she told me, and she wasn't joking.

It didn't stop there. For the rest of the pregnancy, there would be no more sex! Not only that, I should also start looking for another place to sleep because, according to old Chinese teachings, I am forbidden from entering the bedroom altogether.

"You are born in the year of the tiger, and because tigers are dangerous to humans, you can have a very dangerous and even lethal influence on the fetus," I was told. No more *Teach me Tiger* in this household!

It seems that doctors in China generally do not recommend sex during pregnancy, however, if you are not exactly Long John Silver, and let's face it, most of us aren't, then it should be fine. The only obstacle left is to overcome 5,000 years of inherited maternity culture and old wives tales, and of course, you'll have to convince her too, and that might be the hard part.

I don't think a lot of sex is being had among expecting Chinese couples anyway, and many couples seem to abstain completely during pregnancy. One of the reasons behind this is that the Chinese say that pregnant women should avoid having anyone touching or tapping them, especially on the shoulder, as this is considered unlucky (This could be just a little bit difficult to avoid altogether during the night). It becomes just easier to avoid any touching at all. I don't know exactly why this is, but it could be because according to Traditional Chinese Medicine, there are some acupuncture points in the shoulder which are said to be related to premature births. The main reason for not having sex, however, apparently is a strong belief that sex can hurt the baby.

As far as I'm aware, most doctors in the West agree that intercourse cannot reach, touch or harm the baby, and here are a few facts that should validate this: Seven layers of skin protect the baby in your wife's belly. Her cervix has lengthened and hardened to prevent anything from getting into the uterus. Furthermore, her cervix is producing mucous to keep the vagina clean and infection-free. On top of this she has bones, fat, muscles, intestines, and the uterus which all helps to protect the unborn child. To injure a baby in the womb takes a significant amount of force. Most cases of fetal injury are apparently due to domestic violence (gunshot wounds/stabbing) or car accidents. In any event, not due to sex. But of course, I am not an expert, so who am I to argue against thousands of years of deeply held beliefs?

When Chinese doctors do allow pregnant couples to have sex, it seems they usually recommend abstinence for the first and the last three months, and if you absolutely must, then always use a condom. I am sorry, but that really takes all the fun out of pregnancy sex, and I was rather very selfishly looking forward to nine months of unprotected, spontaneous sex. My hopes were up because I had seen that English language pregnancy websites and books usually have several pages or even a whole chapter dedicated to sex during pregnancy, often with helpful illustrations of recommended positions.

With the wife pregnant, many Westerners might consider this a good time to go out looking for a larger apartment or a house with an extra room for the baby, but please be careful here. Do not visit houses which have been left vacant for a long time. Such premises have not been "cleansed" and therefore might be full of evil spirits and ghosts that can affect both you and your baby.

If that wasn't enough, the pregnancy will also affect your social life.

"From now on", Fu told me, "there is no more coming home late from a night out with friends. The Chinese believe that evil spirits come out after midnight and they prefer to roam in the dark."

She also had had to be especially careful to avoid the dark shadows cast by trees as these places are said to be the favourite hiding spots of evil spirits. And as a precaution, to protect the unborn baby from evil spirits, pregnant women are advised to place a knife under their bed. At the same time, many Chinese I know believe that empty beds attract ghosts to sleep on, and therefore, as a precaution, often place little dolls or numerous teddy bears on top of their beds.

In China, most people look out for themselves and mind their own business. They usually don't meddle in the lives of complete strangers, although, face or no face, they will be happy to stare from a short distance. But once Fu got pregnant, she and the fetus all of a sudden became everybody's concern and even responsibility. Without exception, they saw it as their duty and right to tell her what to eat and what not to eat, what kind of clothes and shoes she should wear etc. Shop assistants even refused to sell her certain products if they believed that they could potentially be unhealthy for her or the fetus. Fu was prevented from buying everything from nail polish to medicine.

One evening when I came home from work, Fu told me she had gone to buy a pair of knickers.

"The shop assistant wouldn't sell me the one's I wanted, " she said.

"Why not?" I asked.

"Those are not for pregnant women," the girl in the shop said, "I will sell you these instead,", and my wife showed me a pair of skin-coloured, oversized Bridget Jones' style knickers.

The next thing you will notice is that the walls of your home are now plastered with images and posters of cute and cuddly babies and toddlers. This is in the hope that you will have a beautiful child.

Under normal circumstances, young Chinese women are generally sophisticated and stylish and very concerned with their appearance. On numerous occasions, I have even met Chinese women with full makeup, wearing high-heels and short skirts on a steep mountain path or out trekking on the wild Great Wall. In other words, many would be caught dead without their high-heels and mascara. But once pregnant, they change completely. As mentioned above, the unofficial uniform for pregnant Chinese women seems to be oversized overalls featuring some kind of cute and cuddly teddy bear on the front as well as short hairstyles (some say this is because the hair may take nutrition needed for the baby). Should the mother choose not to undertake this change, she will most likely be frowned-upon.

Fu said 'no' from the start to both teddy bears and short hair so she of course came under fire. She mostly dressed in what in the West is most common for pregnant women, namely dresses that accentuate rather than hide the growing belly. Oh my, how this style garnered disapproving looks and loud comments! While walking on the street one summer afternoon, a middle aged woman with a purple perm and a very concerned look on her face stopped and said to Fu: "You should not wear this kind of dress. It does not allow the child to grow properly!" We were both left dumbstruck.

What should she have been wearing?

Time and time again, I have seen this metamorphosis take place, both at home in our neighbourhood and in the office building where I work. Well before you can actually see anything sticking out, pregnant women will start wearing this god-awful outfit to protect the baby from the supposed harmful effects of radiation from any electrical devices such as mobile phones, computers, and microwave ovens.

I couldn't help but ask a pregnant colleague wearing such a dress about the new addition to her wardrobe. She explained that hidden inside the apron lay a metal mesh that protected her unborn child from the dangerous radiation coming from her computer.

"Ah, I see…" I replied, still rather mystified. But of course a "congratulations" to the lucky lead-lined anti-radiation smock-wearing pregnant colleague was now appropriate.

The World Health Organization says that there is no major risk from using computers or any other electronics around pregnant women, but it seems that the WHO has no authoritative status in China.

An entire industry of "protective" maternity clothing has thrived in China for over two decades as millions of young expectant mothers have spent up to RMB 1,500 (around US$250) on horrendous looking anti-electromagnetic radiation aprons. They seem to be just as necessary for a modern-day pregnancy in China as vitamins and iron tablets. Clever and manipulative companies market these things to protect against everything from miscarriages and insomnia to cardiovascular disease and leukaemia. They even claim that they protect against getting white hair and high blood pressure. All, apparently, in the blissful absence of any scientific evidence. As a matter of fact, a Chinese study showed that even if a woman is wearing an anti-radiation smock, radiation can still enter her body through parts not protected by the clothing, such as the arms, causing the anti-radiation shielding to trap the radiation and increase it to dangerously high levels. Not surprisingly these findings created a storm on Weibo, China's Twitter, with nearly 2 million comments posted in the days after it was made public.

Of all the things pregnant Chinese women should worry about… I don't think I would rank radiation as one of my top concerns. In fact, our Chinese friends and acquaintances who have been wearing these outfits were quite surprised when they learned that expectant mothers in the West have never even heard of these modern 'scientific' dresses, much less worn them.

I read somewhere about a pregnant Chinese woman in Switzerland who asked her Swiss gynaecologist where she could buy an anti-radiation suit. She expected the Swiss to be at the top of scientific development in all aspects, but her doctor had never heard of them. He went on to tell her that the amount of radiation emitted from a computer was less than that from the sun's rays. She then left rather disappointed, but the story unfortunately didn't mention if she ended up buying a suit or not.

Everywhere we went, people would give us advice on things to do, or more often NOT to do during the pregnancy. It is a little like having millions of loudspeakers blasting out Chairman Mao quotations all around you from morning to night, only the slogans were not from the little red book, but rather from 5,000 years of collective Chinese guilt-producing "common sense" mantras, passed down from generation to generation. The effect, I think, is surely something like that rumor about how the U.S. military uses multiple loudspeakers constantly playing loud and repetitive messages 24-7 to encourage prisoners being interrogated to talk.

We started to feel a little bit like that because everywhere we went someone would criticize Fu for not doing this or that, and on top of all that, doing any kind of sports or exercise now turned out to be almost impossible.

Most people in China seem to agree that you should not move at all during your pregnancy. Doing anything that involves any exertion whatsoever, even raising your arms above your head, is frowned upon. Fu, however, was a little inspired from abroad where she heard that exercise would be really good for her. While cycling when pregnant is not officially banned in China, as it is in Japan, it is still very much frowned upon. The supposed danger lies in a combination of the risk of harming the fetus in case of an accident, and the very intense physical strain needed to ride a bicycle (even though I have to say that the normal speed with which the majority of people ride at in China will not likely cause any strain whatsoever). Of course, as everyone who has been in China for a while will know, once the baby is out, bicycling or even motor biking with several children standing between the legs of a parent, or the mother sitting on the back with a baby in her arms (no one wearing a helmet of any kind, one or more are on the phone, and at least one person trying to hold an umbrella because it is either raining or too sunny), is just fine. No one, except me, even turns their head at such a spectacle. But had she been pregnant, it would have been a whole other story.

Fu, even though she hails from mountainous Chongqing,

which happens to be pretty much the only city in China where nobody bicycles, bicycled everywhere until the very end of her pregnancy, and had to listen to numerous warnings and even scoldings.

Next, Fu decided to go swimming. That turned out to be rather more difficult than she had imagined. We went together to the pool, Fu obviously with child, and she only succeeded in swimming one and a half laps before she was approached by no less than three life guards with terrified looks on their faces, who all asked her to get out of the water. Swimming could be dangerous when she was pregnant, they said, and nobody there wanted to take responsibility for her. Two employees led her all the way into the shower, after which, the manager told her that in the future she would have to call first if she wanted to come and swim. He would then make sure that nobody else was in the pool and only then could she come by. However, reading between the lines, it was clear that he did not want her to return. We didn't bother testing it.

After that she started yoga classes, which fortunately didn't result in any strangers' interference. After all, I do think that sitting or lying down or not doing any exercise at all during the whole pregnancy, is much more harmful to the woman, especially considering all the muscles she will eventually need for the tough job of giving birth. Anyway, just my humble opinion...

Our friendly neighbors, the Li's and the Hao's, always greeted us with the common polite phrases, stating the very obvious, like *"chu qu le!* (going out!), *"hui lai le!"* (coming back!), to which they'd never expect any real answer. But now the common greeting among friends especially in Beijing, *"Chi le ma?"*, meaning "Have you eaten?" suddenly required an elaborate answer every time we met them. Being pregnant, Fu of course had to think much more carefully about what she ate. Unsurprisingly, the food-obsessed Chinese have plenty of good advice up their sleeves concerning this. Actually, superstitions aside, I think that we, in the West, could learn a fair bit from the holistic approach to eating and just great knowledge about food that the Chinese have.

One night, as we were standing in front of the gate of our traditional Beijing courtyard, the local cat lady cycled by and just as she passed us she exclaimed, "Remember to eat walnuts now. This is the time when the child grows hair."

Before we even had time to turn around, she was gone. Walnuts look like the human brain, thus it is said they are good for the development of the child's brain, and, according to the cat lady, also the hair.

On the other hand, there were some foods that Fu now had to abstain from. Rabbit heads are a big delicacy in Sichuan, where she comes from. But since becoming pregnant, there must be absolutely no more munching on these little furry friends, her mother told her. The idea is that if you eat rabbit heads while you are pregnant, the child will be born with a cleft lip, because the character for this animal (兔-*tu*) appears in the Chinese term for cleft lip (兔唇-*tuchun*). Squid and crab are also to be avoided. The former because it can cause the uterus to stick during labor, and the latter because it will result in a naughty child. The list goes on and on. Bananas will cause miscarriage, asthma, and speech defects; papaya causes jaundice and a difficult birth; the lychee is too heaty (*yang*), while eating lamb or mutton might cause epilepsy. Dark liquids such as soy sauce, chocolate, cola, coffee and tea will make the baby's skin dark, so as most everyone is obsessed with white and pale skin to a degree that some Chinese girls, at least to my eyes, are almost "see-through" pale approaching the likes of a corpse, that is of course to be avoided at all costs. Pregnant women should also avoid eating snake, geese and shrimp, because they are thought to give the baby bad skin.

And then you have all the "cold" (*yin*) food which to an average foreigner is something of a strange concept to fathom. To make one thing clear, we are not talking about the temperature, but rather the concept that food can create a warming or cooling effect on the body. Cold foods eaten early in pregnancy can lead to premature birth or miscarriage so avoid watermelon, banana and anything containing mung beans at all cost. However, eating these same foods close to the due date can bring about an easy labour.

Finally, there are some things you *should* eat. Sweet black sesame soup is one of them, and a prime choice for expecting mothers, not just because its richness can satisfy any food craving. This thick, warm dessert is supposed to help the baby grow strong bones and dark eyes. I wonder how it doesn't also cause dark skin? I guess not all superstitions are supposed to be coherent.

On a serious note, studies have shown that it is actually a problem in China that pregnant women eat too much during pregnancy while not doing enough exercise, which can cause a difficult delivery.

As the due date was drawing nearer, we started to receive a lot of baby presents from family and friends. Thus the question kept popping up: "How much baby gear should we buy ourselves before the delivery?"

Some Chinese say that keeping baby clothes in the house before the baby is born is bad luck. Also, if we wanted to buy a stroller, we should keep it away from the house and only bring it in after the baby was born, because that too is said to bring bad luck. (We kept our stroller outside just to be on the safe side, and honestly also because there was no room in the house). On top of this, Fu had to stop stroking her stomach because it would lead to a spoiled and very demanding child.

The list would only get longer *after* our first baby was born. I could hardly cope with it anymore. If it had been back in Europe, I probably would have told a number of people to mind their own business, but here I mostly had to accept that this is the way it is, and admire Fu for taking it all so politely. I have had to accept some of the Chinese folk beliefs and Fu decided not to follow all the local advice and instead accepted some of my ideas (a few at least). Our relationship and mutual understanding has become stronger because of the many discussions we have had about what would be best for the baby and I now feel we have managed quite well.

Of course, Fu worried about what her mother, sister-in-law, friends, and even what the not-so-occasional complete stranger told her, and couldn't help but listen to them. She still left the room if I was hammering nails into the walls, but on the other hand she knitted a lot of clothes for our baby and at the end of the day neither our social life, nor indeed sex life, suffered too much...

However, not much of this advice can be measured and proven, but who can say for sure what is simply superstition and what is just common sense? I am no longer so sure myself and it can't hurt to listen to some good and benign advice even if it does come from people you've never met before. And why take any chances? Before our first child Luka was born, I decided that I would rather be on the safe side. After all, he was "Made in China".

Good thing that it was almost time to go to the hospital.

How many pregnant Chinese women actually follow all these

superstitions? To be honest, and not surprisingly, I don't know. Apart from the fact that most of our Chinese and a few foreign friends in China all have abided at least partly to a large number of the taboos. But to get an idea of the practice outside our circle of friends, I have chosen to list a number of the answers given in a Hong Kong study, done among 827 mostly well-educated mothers-to-be, published the year Luka was born. The women here were encouraged to follow a list of over 75 superstitions believed to protect them and their baby during the pregnancy. Here is a selection of some of the superstitions or taboos which the women totally or partially had kept to during those nine long months.

Not eating snake (92%),
Not drinking herbal tea (91%)
Not jumping (89%)
Not wearing high-heeled shoes (84%)
No hammering of nails, no wall drilling, no home renovation, and no dismantling/moving beds and moving heavy objects (80-84%).
No iced food (83%)
No crab (82%)
No rabbit meat (79%)
No walking too fast (73%)
No sexual intercourse (68%)
No usage of needles/scissors in bed (66%)
No hugging of children (53%)
No hand-raising (52%)
Not allowing children to jump on pregnant woman's bed (33%)
Do not use broken bowls or cups (24%)
Do not break soy sauce containers (19%)

Conceal ugly toys (18%)
Only change bedding on lucky days (11%)

Why did they do it, you might ask? The reasons why these urban Hong Kong women followed the taboos despite their educational background, was primarily for the sake of the baby, secondly for their own sake, and only thirdly to calm down the family.

Even though the family came last, more than 60 percent of the women had felt that they either had lost some of their freedom, felt unhappy about the restrictions or had argued with the family regarding the observation of the superstitions. For these women, the taboos and superstitions became a significant stress factor during the pregnancy and led to a higher number of women with depression later on both before and after the delivery.

7

BLUE OR PINK?

> *When a son is born,*
> *Let him sleep on the bed,*
> *Clothe him with fine clothes,*
> *And give him jade to play...*
> *When a daughter is born,*
> *Let her sleep on the ground,*
> *Wrap her in common wrappings,*
> *And give broken tiles to play...*
> From the Book of Songs (1000–700 B.C.)

From when Fu was about eight weeks pregnant, almost everybody, with a high degree of authority and conviction, had decided upon the baby's sex. From her parents and their friends, to our friends and acquaintances, our cleaning lady, the neighbors, and the local fruit and vegetable seller, right through to complete strangers who stopped us on the street, everyone seemed to know if it was a boy or a girl. There was not a single shred of doubt in their voices or expressions. "Your stomach is pointed so you will have a boy", or, "great that you will have a girl first, so she can take care of the boy who will come as number two."

There was far from a consensus, although as the pregnancy

progressed a larger proportion told us it would be a boy. One night when we went for a walk, an old grey-haired Chinese gentleman carrying a great black walking cane, mostly for looks, I think, came towards us and out of the blue, said, "You will have a boy. Congratulations!" Afterwards he added, "Don't ask why, I just know and I have never been wrong." Then he continued on his way, and left us standing there, speechless. But, after all, he was right!

"I think you should prepare blue baby clothes...", said the doctor in almost a whisper after some hesitation, in answer to my question if it was a "little sister" or "little brother" that we were expecting. In recent years before Luka was born it had become increasingly difficult to find out if you were getting a boy or a girl, and even though as a foreigner you are not part of China's one-child-policy family planning, doctors are not officially allowed to tell you. However, there are of course ways around this, as the example above shows. Ultrasonic screening to determine an infant's sex, as well as sex-selective abortion, was banned in China in 1989. Although this law was of course not made for us in particular, you just can't help thinking, do they really imagine that we would choose not to have the baby if we were told it was a girl? To a Westerner, is it hard to imagine that a simple question like asking the sex of the fetus would have to be so difficult to answer. But as a direct result of the "one-child policy" (which was relaxed in 2015 allowing couples to have two children) that had been imposed on the Chinese population back in 1979 and the continuance of preferring sons over daughters (*zhong nan qing nü*), since then resulting in nearly 350 million abortions primarily of female fetus', and more than 40 million young bachelors unable to find a bride, China is today in dire need of girls.

BLUE OR PINK?

In 2011, on a summer trip to the former German colony, Qingdao, in Shandong province, to escape the sweltering summer heat of China's capital, we all stayed in a faded antiquated villa in the old town, which admittedly had seen better days. The massive bells of the impressive Protestant church, designed in the Romanesque and Jugendstil styles of Kaiser Wilhelm's Germany which stood across the street, woke us up early every morning. The city's fame include picturesque beaches, and fresh Tsingtao beer (often sold in plastic bags with a straw), so, while we did visit the old brewery, most of the days we spent on the famous sandy beaches on the Qingdao coast.

These beaches are, unfortunately, also some of the most crowded in the world, so securing a spot on Beach No. 1 to enjoy the sun-drenched stretches of sand or the refreshing, turquoise waters of the Yellow Sea, was no easy task. Finally seated in the shade under the protection of a rented parasol, a throng of locals surrounded us. Many of the Chinese women, fixated by keeping their pale, almost translucent complexion, which is the beauty ideal (which also makes it near to impossible to buy a skin cream without a *meibai*, whitening effect), dressed in full body swaths of UV-protective mesh in all sorts of floral designs. To be on the safe side, some even wore the infamous, locally invented, "facekini": a spandex mask stretched over the head with holes for the nose, mouth, and eyes offering extreme protection from the scorching sun. It made them look like superheroes; although they were still a far cry from Michelle Pfeiffer as Cat Woman.

The Chinese say that a view of the Qingdao beach during the summer time looks like dumplings boiled in a pot (*zhu jiaozi*). Occasionally, and not to be boiled completely, during siesta we had to retreat to the villa from the masses, to catch a breath and a nap, and so miraculously, Fu became pregnant with our second child (who also turned out to be a boy).

When we took Luka to one of the ultrasound scans and tried to tell him that there was a little brother or sister up there on the screen, he insisted there was something wrong with the TV, and kept asking for the remote control. He wanted to turn over to watch Kung Fu Panda instead, which was his absolute favourite cartoon at the time. I must admit I couldn't blame him. In the first half of the pregnancy it can be really difficult to make any sense of the blurry picture (After the first ultrasound, Fu had actually fully convinced me that we were expecting twins when we were looking at the print-out from the hospital) and the noise coming from it when the doctor says, "There is the head, the feet, the hands…can't you see it?" Luka would much rather watch pure awesomeness with THE big, fat Panda! No wonder.

The Chinese have always had a preference for boys. One of my admittedly many hobbies has been collecting old photographs from around China documenting about a hundred and fifty years of change and transformation of China's cities and countryside. Many of the photos have been taken by foreigners while travelling, studying, working or living in China, but I have also collected hundreds of photos taken in Chinese photo studios. Some of my favourite photos are family photos, because in them it is possible to follow the history and development of Chinese society from imperial times to modern days. In them, you can trail the way both fashion and customs changed, but also how modern inventions like bicycles, cars, trains, airplanes and even space rockets made their way in to the family photo.

Nevertheless, it is also noteworthy that the social hierarchies of Chinese society have very much stayed the same even up until this day. In many of these photos, especially the ones from the countryside, the girls are consigned to the fringes of the photograph, since they will be married off anyway, and as such, they are deemed less important. However, the smaller baby boys, often dressed up as girls to confuse the evil spirits, are the centre of attention. It is so important to keep for posterity, that they sit at the front, sometimes held by the mother or grandmother, so their penises proudly stick out of the holes of their open trousers, leaving no one in doubt.

In early 2006, my friend Lars' Chinese teacher, Nongmin, invited us to spend Chinese New Year with him. Nongmin isn't his real name as it means 'farmer' or 'peasant' and in the cities, it is often used as a derogatory term. City people often refer to *nongmin* with contempt and look down upon them as stupid and inferior. However, there is nothing inferior about this *nongmin* at all, or his wife Yumi, a name which means 'corn', and I believe their nicknames are always lovingly used. Nevertheless, Nongmin does indeed come from the countryside and from a long line of farmers.

We travelled together on a train, then a local long-distance bus, and finally a pirate cab (called a "black car" *heiche* in Chinese) before reaching the village of his ancestors in a distant corner of southeastern Hebei, a stone throw from the provinces of Shandong and Henan, and not far from the cradle of Chinese civilization, the Yellow River. It was only about eight or nine hours' travel south from Beijing, but it was an altogether different world. Not only was it freezing cold everywhere, outside as well as inside, as the front door of Nongmin's childhood home was always open, and nearly impossible to understand the local dialect, but it was also the heartland of the Chinese countryside on the North China plain and as such very traditional and conservative. It was also in this area that the infamous and ultra conservative Boxer Rebellion first saw light around the year of 1898.

It was a bleak and desolate landscape, everything was grey and brown and dust blew in from all around, covering the village, the few poplar trees and the walled courtyard in a thick layer. Apart from the pride of the village, the new pig farm, which really was such an unpleasant place to visit that I swore I wouldn't eat pork anymore, the area had clearly missed out on the Chinese economic miracle. Nongmin's relatives had recently refurbished the brick house and it now had a large main room with the wooden beams visible above, heated only by a small coal stove, around which everybody huddled. In one corner was a voluminous sofa still covered in plastic and in the other a new homemade wooden plank bed where all the men slept. This had replaced the old, but definitely more comfortable *kang*, which is the heated bed-cum-sofa raised brick platform common in the countryside of northern China. The women all slept in an adjacent room. The lavatory (a hole in the ground) was still in the courtyard, only halfway covered behind a mud wall about one meter tall and right next to the pigsty.

As a complete contrast, Nongming's family and relatives were a lovely and joyful bunch and they did everything to make us feel at home. However, I was surprised to see how separated the men and women were in their everyday lives. Nongming's female cousin, about ten years his junior, was always either cleaning or in the kitchen preparing food. Although she was only seventeen years old, she looked at least thirty or more, her face already worn with wrinkles by the hard life in the countryside. Dressed in about five layers of worn cotton-padded clothes and cooking sleeves, her hands and face were red and swollen from frostbites, and her hands and fingers so thick she handled the heavy scorching hot iron wok with her bare hands straight from the wood-fired stove. She had never travelled outside of the province, but they were already talking about her future marriage. (Even though the official age requirement for marriage is twenty for women in China, in the countryside they often marry earlier).

While we lounged around, me as close to the coal stove as possible, with the other men snacking on watermelon seeds, sweets and sipping tea, and chain smoking, the women busied themselves by continuously serving new refreshments, pouring hot water, and sweeping the floor. At mealtimes, they served us first and then only ate afterwards at a different table in their bedroom. It was the same everywhere we went in the village. The boys and men didn't do anything.

As we were some of the first foreigners to visit the village since the French Catholic missionaries had left the area just before the communists took control of China in 1949, word quickly spread. Many locals turned up at all hours of the day to meet and greet us, and after a while, it became rather tiring being the 'monkey' in the cage and having no privacy.

To get away for the day, and to do some research for a book I was working on, we decided to go for Sunday mass at the century-old Catholic church in the county town of Handan. Although Nongming's relatives weren't Catholics, the whole area was under a strong influence from the church and faith. It looked out of place, but on every other gate, a defining and rather exclusive statement was written in large characters: "We belong to the Catholic church". The church was completely cramped with people down to the very last seat, with men seated to the left and women to the right. Just like in the area between Christians and non-Christians, the men and women were likewise segregated. However, soon many people fell asleep during the priest's long and condemning speech, only wakening for a short while, when he took the thick and heavy old bible and smashed it down on his pulpit to awaken his slumbering congregation.

After we had celebrated a great New Year's eve with more than enough food and *baijiu*, lots of fireworks, and a Chinese opera performance in the village, we spent the next day visiting Nongming's relatives and more snacks and tea followed. We left after some days, because I had succumbed to a vicious flu. It had been a great eye-opening experience, but I was so happy to be back in my own heated courtyard house in Beijing again. Here, only my sweet but very curious next-door neighbour, my landlords' mother, Mrs Hao, would watch my every move and often walk in unannounced. But as in most other Chinese families I got to know in Beijing, she was very much the one wearing the pants in the family and nobody told her what to do or what to say. The difference between the city and the countryside in China is astounding.

On a research trip to Dandong in Liaoning, on the border with North Korea, I met a young girl named "*Zhaodi*", meaning to call for a little brother because the character for little brother, and wife of a younger brother, are both pronounced "*di*". The Chinese character is actually a combination of the character for girl and little brother. She explained to me that it was quite a common name in the countryside, as her parents, like most others, wanted boys. To the relief of her parents it had apparently worked because she had a younger brother. This age old preference for boys is due to both traditional Confucian values such as filial piety and the belief that male heirs are necessary to carry on the family name and, crucially, to take care of their parents in the afterlife so their spirits do not wander the Earth as hungry ghosts. But it is also for practical reasons like inheritance of land, and, more importantly, sons are expected to take care of the parents in their old age. China even made filial piety part of a new law in 2013 resulting in numerous court cases where neglected parents have filed cases against their children.

BLUE OR PINK?

The good news is that from around 2009 to 2012 the ratio of girls to boys became more equal, but it still was 117 boys for every 100 girls (down from 120 at the time of the Beijing Olympics), and in 2015 it was still at nearly 114. However, it is still a far cry from the global natural sex ratio at birth which is commonly assumed to be around 105 boys to 100 girls. In China, the boy-girl balance tends to be normal in cities, but in rural areas the sex ratio at birth could be 130 or even 150 boys to every 100 girls. In some rural areas where the problem is particularly acute, kindergarten classes can have twenty or so boys and maybe only three girls. In many primary schools there are enough boys to fill five classes but only enough girls for two.

For Luka, it was rather obvious that what we were seeing on the ultrasound was not a bean sprout between his legs, and the doctor just looked at me when I asked her, "Is that what I think it is?" She even let the ultrasound device linger for a little while longer to leave no doubt, and asked us, "Well, what do you think?"

Anyway, when my German friend Constanze was at her ultrasound scan around six months into her pregnancy, the doctor at a private hospital in Beijing also refused to tell her the sex of the fetus. To get around this, my friend told the doctor that, in her country, it was considered extremely good luck to know beforehand. The tactics worked and the doctor succumbed and told them. You cannot deliberately deny somebody good fortune, after all.

Morgan, another Italian-American friend of mine, had to go in three times before the doctor finally told him it was a girl. "I went in three times to ask her, the third time was a charm. I think it helped that I went in to speak with her alone, without Ling [his wife], when no one was around. If I was Chinese, she wouldn't have told me."

According to an article I read on a Chinese internet forum, a couple from the countryside had tested a method to make sure that the wife would deliver a boy. Apparently, it was fool proof. They had for months placed a piece of metal underneath one of their hens in the chicken coop and all that came out of the eggs were roosters. Accordingly the peasant woman placed a hammer underneath her bed during her pregnancy and after nine months, she gave birth to a boy. It should be a true story! Less sure about the logic…

Boy or girl? Actually, we could have decided on the sex of the child ourselves. Haihai, Fu's sister in law, said: "If you want a boy, you should eat tofu, mushrooms, noodles, and salad. If you want a girl, then you should eat pickles, meat and fish."

In general, sour or salty food will produce boys, while sweet or spicy food will produce girls. But as I mentioned in the beginning, it hasn't really worked for us.

The words of a doctor or the prophecies of complete strangers are actually redundant because the Chinese have an ancient method by which you can calculate whether you will have a boy or a girl. Using the 700-year old 'Chinese Pregnancy Calendar' you can, apparently, discover the sex of your child just by knowing which month the baby was conceived, together with the age of the mother. A quick look at this chart could have told us immediately what we later learned from the ultrasound scan– namely that it was a boy. Luka was conceived in January, and Fu was 37. (It was less perfect for Luka's younger brother, Louis, our second child, though…)

Try it for yourself.

The process of pregnancy is a kind of magic, it really is. Your wife's body will swell in many ways and areas that you probably never considered were pregnancy-related before. Most men will

Chinese Pregnancy Calendar

First, try to remember when the actual conception took place, and locate the month on the left-hand column, then match it to the mother's age when the child was conceived. Follow the coordinates to their intersection and note the result. Boy or girl?

	Maternal Age																											
Month	18	19	20	21	22	23	24	25	26	27	28	29	30	31	32	33	34	35	36	37	38	39	40	41	42	43	44	45
January	F	M	F	M	F	M	M	F	M	F	M	F	M	M	M	F	M	M	F	M	F	M	F	M	F	M	M	F
February	M	F	M	F	M	M	F	M	F	M	F	M	F	F	M	M	F	M	M	F	M	F	M	F	M	F	M	M
March	F	M	F	F	F	F	M	M	F	M	F	M	F	M	M	M	M	F	F	M	F	M	F	M	M	M	F	M
April	M	F	M	M	F	M	M	F	F	F	F	F	F	M	M	F	F	M	F	F	M	M	M	F	M	F	M	F
May	M	F	M	M	M	F	M	F	F	F	M	F	F	F	F	F	F	F	M	F	M	F	M	F	M	F	M	F
June	M	M	F	M	F	F	M	F	F	M	M	F	F	F	F	F	F	F	F	M	F	F	M	M	M	F	M	F
July	M	M	F	F	F	F	F	M	M	M	M	M	F	F	F	F	M	F	F	F	M	M	F	M	M	F	M	M
August	M	M	M	F	F	F	F	M	M	M	M	M	F	F	F	F	F	M	F	M	F	M	F	M	M	F	M	F
September	M	M	F	F	M	M	F	F	M	F	M	F	F	F	F	M	M	M	M	F	M	F	F	M	M	M	F	M
October	M	M	F	F	M	F	M	F	F	F	M	F	M	F	F	F	F	F	M	M	F	M	F	M	F	M	M	F
November	M	F	F	M	F	M	F	M	F	M	F	F	M	M	M	M	M	M	M	F	M	F	M	F	M	M	F	M
December	M	F	M	F	F	M	F	M	F	M	F	F	M	M	M	M	M	M	M	F	F	F	F	M	F	M	F	M

probably think big breasts and wide hips (just like the title of Mo Yan's famous novel) now...but that's not all that will be big, I should say!

Fu's nose did start swelling, but not as much as some of our Chinese friends and relatives. A friend of ours, I choose to call her Li Jing, her nose really, and I mean REALLY, swelled up. However, the Chinese have a saying: "*Huai nanhai hui bianchou, huai nühai hui bian piaoliang*", which should have given us yet another clue as to the sex of the baby. It means, "While pregnant with a boy you will become ugly; while pregnant with a girl you will become pretty". And although neither Fu or Li Jing turned ugly during their pregnancies (they actually both had that beautiful pregnancy glow), the fact is that by the end of the day they both gave birth to a son.

Luckily, especially for men, other body parts start to swell as well. Maybe you are one of those men (I am thinking the majority) who have been expecting and maybe also waiting eagerly for the day your wife's breasts start growing. You just can't miss it. In Fu's case it started right away, and within the first two months they had grown a full cup size. And it doesn't have to stop there. They could be tempting to touch, but don't dare risk it. However tempting they might look, they are also extremely sensitive, tender and even painful–so you might not be allowed to touch at all.

Luckily all this swelling will–eventually–most of the time–return to its normal, pre-pregnancy glory! It may not, however, happen overnight. Overall now was the time to be careful. You won't be the first man to think your pregnant wife has gone crazy. When all her feelings seem like they are on the outside, then now is the time to stand up and get into character as a supportive husband and future father.

BLUE OR PINK?

I like to think most of my male friends keep an imaginary goodwill account or box (I am pretty convinced they do), otherwise also known as 'building up brownie points', 'drinking tickets' etc. somewhere in their relationship with their partner. How many of their girlfriends and wives actually have any knowledge of this or even keep their own account, I really don't know. Every man has his own way of filling up the box, some more misguided than others. The account can be supplemented with back rubs, foot massages, doing the dishes, calling her mother, velvety red roses, Swiss chocolate or with more elaborate gifts, such as jewelry, expensive perfume, beautiful dresses, candlelight dinners...you name it, and the goodwill account fills up.

The payback is nights out with the guys in the local bar, sports games, Tour de France and World Cup on TV and probably also a wish for something more....As Sheldon in The Big Bang Theory puts it: "Interesting. Sex works even better than chocolate to modify behaviour. I wonder if anyone else has stumbled onto that?". If you are one of those guys with an imaginary goodwill account, you will know what I am talking about. The point is, after your wife becomes pregnant and later on, after the baby is born, don't count on it working like it used to for at least two to three years, if ever again. For your own sake, you might as well put a sign on the box, saying "temporarily out of order"!

With all that swelling, and even with foot massages, Fu was starting to feel a little like an elephant and just wished for the pregnancy to be over with, the sooner the better. We both simply just wanted a new birthday to celebrate in our little family.

We got a birthday alright, but not the one we had been wishing for...

8

Happy Birthday

As some of you probably know, The People's Republic of China was founded on October 1, 1949. Thus October 1, 2009 was Communist China's sixtieth anniversary. In China, sixty years is traditionally one of the most important birthday celebrations, so this of course would not go unnoticed and would most certainly be celebrated. Not only would it be celebrated, no matter what got in the way-say costs or security-it would go down in history as one of China's largest parades to date. And I should add that China is known for some pretty large parades.

Living in Beijing during the massive preparations for the 2008 Olympics, as well as other large celebrations such as the return of Hong Kong in 1997, it was clear that this time both preparations and precautions far exceeded those undertaken for past events. Although this was a celebration (read: demonstration of power and might by the Communist Party), for the Chinese, very few "people", much less those living close by the parade area, were actually invited to watch the parade. We were living just five minutes away in an old *hutong* neighbourhood on the east side of the Forbidden City, and if we had expected an invitation to join in the celebrations, we would definitely have waited in vain. As a matter of fact, all the residents in our small neighbourhood were instructed not to come out or even look at the rehearsals, during

HAPPY BIRTHDAY

which tanks and armoured personnel carriers rumbled past our otherwise peaceful little enclave on their way to, ironically enough, Chang'an Jie, the 'Avenue of Eternal Peace'.

Rehearsals for the big day started months earlier, more often than not paralyzing transportation in large areas of the capital. Several times, I tried to return home on my bike, but had to patiently wait until thousands of schoolchildren with their small blue and green plastic stools (for sitting on during hours of waiting), or thousands of troops from the People's Liberation Army, or hundreds of green battle tanks had passed. During the rehearsal sessions, squads of SWAT police dressed in black bulletproof vests and heavily armed, paramilitary and security forces with armoured cars, were placed all along the parade roads and intersections. On top of this, thousands of "volunteers" (mostly elderly people from the neighbourhood committees said to have numbered more than 800,000) with their new red armbands, stood by nervously, wanting to make absolutely sure that nothing went wrong on their watch. At the same time, fighter planes rehearsed their anniversary show above our heads. It was like living in the middle of a war zone.

As a foreigner, I was lucky in some ways. I only had to show my passport with a valid visa and a matching residence permit and I was okay. Meaning that I could get in and out of our neighbourhood without too many problems. It was an altogether different story for Fu. Not only was she an outsider, a *waidiren*, without a Beijing *hukou* or even an official permit to reside in Beijing, much less a Beijing employee, the chances of staying in Beijing during the extravaganza were slim to none. And if this was not enough, at this point she was heavily pregnant with a due date in late October.

The security was so tight that the local government had even prohibited the flying of domesticated pigeons over the center of the capital. Kite-flying was also temporarily banned. My old time friend and enthusiastic master of kite-making and kite-flying, Mr Wang, was a little annoyed that he had to stop his daily kite flying activities, but, as he said, *"mei banfa"*–What can I do about it?"

In order for us to "fix" the problem with Fu staying in the capital, we had to visit the local public security bureau, usually known in English as the PSB. She needed to have issued and stamped a local registration document in order for her to legally stay in the city. First time over to the PSB with our marriage certificates in hand, we were told that without a local job, Fu would have to travel back to Chengdu, where she had both her work unit (*danwei*) and residence permit. They simply would neither issue much less stamp anything.

We went back home feeling almost like giving up. If Fu was not to be sent back, we had to find a viable solution. She went back to the PSB later that day with our landlord, and luckily the officer who had previously denied issuing the correct documents was either out for lunch or in the toilet. Either way, his colleague issued and stamped everything and so they left in a hurry before the ink was dry.

A little later, Fu had asked one of the other local policemen, "What if I go into labour during one of the rehearsals or on the day of the anniversary celebrations itself?"

"Move to a hotel room far away from here," was his reply. The celebrations were still a month away…

One night we went out for a nice Indian meal and afterwards to listen to some Mongolian throat singing in Beijing's cosy Nanluogu Xiang alleyway, and (going against all the Chinese beliefs about evil spirits in dark places during the night) it was around 11pm before we started heading home. We did not get far, however, because we were stopped just south of the alley by

HAPPY BIRTHDAY

police and hundreds of rumbling green tanks which were having rehearsals around Tiananmen Square and were now heading back to the barracks. We simply had to wait it out.

A local Chinese man who might have had a few too many that evening was pacing up and down the sidewalk beside us. He apparently did not have much patience, and started to make loud complaints. All of a sudden he ran out and tried to cross the road in between two battle tanks. Both police and volunteers ran after him, jumped on him and nailed him to the ground, and then dragged him back onto the sidewalk. One of the volunteers now spent the next twenty minutes pointing fingers and scolding him at the same time. An hour and a half later we were finally allowed to go home. Maybe there is something about those evil spirits after all...

Finally, on the day of celebration itself, when fog and clouds had miraculously dispersed overnight, we watched on the TV as president Hu Jintao cruised past more than a 100,000 troops, including helmeted jet pilots and policewomen in white go-go boots and short red skirts, and some 10,000 school children waving coloured placards, along with battle tanks, attack helicopters, cruise missiles and other heavy toys. It was all happening only five or ten minutes away, and yet we were not allowed to watch it.

Driving out from beneath the Gate of Heavenly Peace, where Mao had declared the foundation of the People's Republic of China exactly 60 years earlier, President Hu Jintao was standing inside his open-roofed Red Flag limousine, only half of him visible, in his grey Mao tunic, and shouting over and over again, "*Tongzhimen hao. Tongzhimen xinkule*"-"Hello comrades! Comrades, hard work!"), and in unison, the troops replied: "Hello Commander!" and "Serve the people!" Very few people use the communist term "comrade" anymore, unless jokingly, and funnily enough, the term is more often used in its other connotation, which just happens to be "gay"! Altogether, it seemed like not much had changed since the late 1950s. It was still good old communist-realist kitsch, though very impressive. And although the parade had a modern twist with a few wind turbines on top of one of the hundreds of floats passing by the members of the watching politburo, sitting on the balcony atop the old gate into the Forbidden City, it still reminded me much more of the mass games seen in North Korea, China's Northeastern neighbour, than a modern superpower.

Like our old neighbour Mr Hao would always say, "They put up red banners with slogans in gold and white, and everything is turned upside down; and then one week later everything is back to normal." He was also right this time around, of course. We had all survived the festivities and things were pretty much back to normal again. What was more important, however, was that the birth of our first born baby could be any day now!

9

THE EAGLE HAS LANDED

Or so we thought, anyway. At least we were getting really close, but he was not going to come out without a fight.

One Sunday evening Fu had felt some contractions come and go several times, and as we were just two days away from the due date, we said to ourselves "This is it!" Bags were packed and we were ready to go. But as the contractions passed we went to bed. Then at around two in the morning they came back with a vengeance and we decided to go to the hospital right away. The doctor on duty assured us that we still had to wait some time, but because the amniotic fluid was a little too low, they decided to keep Fu there so we were officially registered and given our 4-star suite in the hospital which we had prepaid for. Later that day, the doctor thought it would be best to try and speed up the process by artificial means. Fu was given labor-stimulating IV drops and then we just had to sit and wait. Luckily there was a DVD player in the room, and we had taken all the seasons of "Shaun the Sheep" with us. It turned out that we would have plenty of time to watch all seasons of our woolly little friend several times over, because although Fu was in terrible pain, nothing much else really happened. At least not for the first few days.

It was of course very frustrating and tough on Fu–both

physically and mentally. When, on the fourth day with labor-stimulating drops, the doctor finally said that this is the last chance before we will give you a C-section, the little boy decided that now would be a good time to come out. So he did, but not without the help of both an epidural for the mother and a ventouse, making it possible to do a vacuum extraction, for him.

On October 29, 2009, at 6 pm, Fu gave birth to a healthy, screaming boy of 4.1kg and 53cm. Luka, as we had decided to call him, was finally born after four hard days of labour. I was both overly happy with joyous tears, but also dumbfounded and mesmerized. Had Fu squeezed too hard or was something wrong with him? To my surprise he looked like a Smurf from behind, on account of having a blue backside, just like he had been hit hard in the bottom. As it turns out, this is exactly what had happened, at least according to the Chinese.

The "Blue Mongolian Ass" (it doesn't have a poetic name in Chinese, most probably because it is so common), as some people call this phenomenon, is caused by *Songzi Niangniang*, the goddess of children, who hits the baby in the behind in 'encouragement' if it is reluctant to get out and face the world. *Songzi Niangniang*, also known as *Zhusheng Niangniang*, "the maiden who brings children", is a Taoist goddess of fertility. She is often depicted as Guanyin (the bodhisattva of compassion) herself and she is worshipped by people who want children, and specifically those who want their child to be a boy. I don't recall doing any worshipping, but maybe I should check with Fu.

Another possibility, and I would like to think of it that way, is that, according to an article in the science magazine, *Discover*, "1 in 200 men are direct descendants of Genghis Khan". The article explains that the existence of these Y chromosomal lineages indicate a periodic 'winner-take-all' dynamic in human genetics more reminiscent of hyper-polygynous mammals such as elephant seals." We simply have to take a DNA ancestry test soon. I just hope that the percentage of Neanderthal is not too high.

In fact the "Mongolian spot" or "blue spot", as it is more commonly known, is very common among non-Caucasians. The term stems from the fact that it was discovered on Japanese children by a German doctor who was the personal physician of the Japanese Emperor. He named it after Mongolians, or rather children of the Mongoloid race. The spots are not only common among Asians, but also among Hispanics, Africans and Native Americans. So I had no need to worry, as it would most likely eventually go away. Some Asians, nonetheless, retain a very small bluish spot for their whole life. However, I quickly forgot about it, because I was immediately faced by a new question or rather dilemma, when the doctor on duty asked, "Do you want to take the placenta home?"

I was close to replying, "No thanks, can I just take the boy, please?" The placenta! I was not prepared for this question. Do I look like Hannibal Lecter? Fu luckily stepped in, and told her that we would pass on this otherwise tempting offer. But more on this later!

Anyway, we were in a private hospital, so the meter was very much running from the moment we set foot inside. Every time the doctor or nurse came for a visit, they would check a box on a big sheet of paper on the wall, as proof that we had received this and that service.

"Do you want local or foreign produced vaccines?" the friendly nurse would ask while she was preparing the syringe.

"Vaccines?" I thought. "He's only just come out." Was there really any choice here? Without saying anything the message from the nurse was clear: you would only choose the local option if you are cheap or simply a bad father. She smiled, and asked me to sign here, here and here.

After a few days I kind of gave up on checking the sheet. Don't get me wrong. The staff was very nice, but it was really difficult to be constantly faced with questions about the health of my wife and child. Call me spoiled, but I would really have liked to leave those kinds of decisions to the doctors, as one would have done in Denmark, and instead have concentrated 100 percent on supporting Fu. However, this is the way it is at most hospitals in China–public as well as private. And after seven days of signing forms, of course choosing the imported medicine every time, wife and child were finally discharged.

It had been almost 25 degrees Celsius when we arrived at the hospital a week earlier. And now it was snowing. Proof again that there really are only two seasons in Beijing: summer and winter.

Driving home in the taxi, I was thinking how close Fu had come to having a C-section. Luckily she did not have to go through that as well, but in most hospitals in China, the doctor would surely have opted for a C-section much earlier. Fu's case was an exception, because in China, Caesareans are simply the choice of the day.

In a country where nearly 50,000 babies are born every day, just over 46 percent of all expectant mothers in China choose to give birth with surgical help. A quarter of these are not medically necessary according to the World Health Organization (WHO). That's a much higher rate than the Asian average of 27 percent (in some Chinese hospitals it is as high as 80 percent). According to the *China Daily*, China has the highest number of C-sections in the world.

In recent years the rate of women having C-sections has risen across the world, but there are significant differences between countries. In the major cities of Brazil, it is as high as 80%, in the US the C-section rate is around 35%, while in Scandinavia it is between 15 and 20%.

One of the reasons for the large percentage of C-sections in China is that many Chinese women and their families believe that if they eat a lot during pregnancy, the baby will be healthy. However, while the baby might still be healthy, the result is that, with their small frames, the babies are simply too large for them to deliver naturally.

A Chinese internet survey in 2013 posed the following question to participants: "Mothers, why are you giving up on natural childbirth?" Some of the answers were perhaps not very different from what you might see in the West, like number 4 on the list: "I'd like to have a natural birth, but I'm afraid it will influence my sex life"; or number 6: "I am of small build so I am not confident I can go through with a natural labour." Other responses were clearly more Chinese, like number 3: "My mother-in-law is superstitious about dates and wants to pick the time of birth." The number one reason on the list, however, was: "When everybody else is having surgery, why should I go through the suffering?"

Around that time, a new Chinese TV-show might even have been stopping some Chinese women from wanting to become pregnant altogether.

With nearly 200 million posts on Weibo (China's Twitter) over just one weekend after its first airing, the reality TV show "*Lai ba haizi*" ("*Come on, Baby*") became an instant hit. The first episode on prime time television featured three women in labour. It is reality TV at its most compelling: one woman was screaming and pulling her hair during labour, while another had a C-section, and the midwife held up the blood-covered new-born in front of the camera. The live show was originally intended for parents to watch with their children, but with graphic scenes such as the ones described, it's no wonder one Chinese parent wrote this on her blog:

"It's just too terrifying. It's even more horrifying than a horror movie. There's a splatter of blood; seeing that knife cut into the abdomen scared me half to death."

Under the hashtag "#Are you brave enough to watch a mother give birth?", another netizen wrote: "…this show will only add to your psychological trauma", and yet another mom-to-be commented: "After watching *Come On, Baby*, I really don't dare to give birth to a baby of my own. […] I was so scared that I cried".

Is watching someone give birth on television a good way to prepare for your own labor and delivery? Who knows, but nobody in China will get another chance for some time at least. After just one episode, the show was taken off the air by the Chinese censors after massive protests from the public.

Fu and I watched it together, and while I have to admit that it was very graphic, there were also funny parts. Especially when one of the fathers had to be continuously asked by the nurse to cut his long pinkie fingernail or he would not be allowed to hold the new born baby. For men in China (I have seen quite a few foreigners with long pinkies too), a long pinkie nail is thought to display higher social standing, indicating that one does not engage in manual labour. By coincidence, Fu and I were in a taxi the next day and the driver had a pinkie nail on his left hand about 10 cm long. He told us it had taken two years to grow, and he was now working on getting his right pinkie just as long. I didn't know what to reply, so I mumbled a "*jiayou*" meaning "go for it". A long pinkie nail can also be a practical and handy tool, equally useful as both booger scoop and earwax excavator.

THE EAGLE HAS LANDED

Even though China's family planning policy, better known as the one child policy, changed in 2015, allowing for couples to have two children, the fact remains that for reasons such as costs, many Chinese couples will probably continue to have only one child. With only one pregnancy and only one childbirth, people don't want to take any risks, and many in China mistakenly believe C-sections to be safer for both mother and child. Furthermore, doctors often do not help to alter that perception because they have their own reasons for recommending Caesareans. One is money. Both the hospital and doctors simply make more money on a Caesarean than a normal delivery. The other one being time. First of all, hospitals can be more efficient with bed occupancy and treat a higher number of patients. But secondly, we have heard from a Chinese friend who is a doctor, that with the C-section the doctors can plan the delivery, meaning that he or she doesn't have to stay for long hours into the night waiting for a baby to finally come out. And finally, doctors are pressured by many prospective parents and their families to opt for a C-section so they can decide the exact time of the delivery.

A Chinese acquaintance–let's call her Jingjing–wanted everything to be perfect. She is wealthy and had everything she wanted, except a child. Under pressure and constant nagging from parents and family, she made a plan. To silence the family she needed a child, but she didn't want a husband. In other words, she needed a donor. However, this wouldn't be easy with all the gossip and loss of face for her and her parents, so she ended up marrying. The plan was to get pregnant and then get a divorce. But Jinging had to wait for the right year to get pregnant, because some years and their corresponding Chinese zodiac animals are considered more fortunate than others.

Like Jingjing, many Chinese couples will wait and try to plan the birth so the child will be born in the year of the dragon, horse or snake, which are considered the most auspicious. It is also generally believed that certain animals get on better with each other than others, thus parents try to plan the right year to give birth in order for the combined sum of animals and their individual characteristics to bring prosperity to the family. Tigers, like myself, are often seen as having a bad temper. But, as mentioned earlier, a friend of mine refers to me as 'Buddha', and I am pretty sure that is because I don't fit in to that category. But it is also said that tigers tend to question authority and therefore are likely to cause trouble for themselves, their family or even to his or her employer at some stage of life. And I am less sure about that one.

The consequences of the Chinese belief in the zodiac animals are not to be underestimated. Over the last 30-40 years, Taiwan, which already has one of the lowest fertility rates in the world, has seen a significant drop in per capita births during tiger years. However, it cannot be all bad, as according to Shaolan Hsueh, the founder of a new way to learn Chinese, called *Chineasy*, the majority out of the Forbes Top 300 of the world's richest people, are born in the year of the tiger. On the other hand it is believed that if you give birth to a son in the year of the rooster, he will be stressed, and if you give birth to a girl in the year of the goat (also called sheep), she will be poor, and have a hard life. Ironically, goats were only second to the tigers on the Forbes list.

The Chinese even have a popular saying that goes: only one out of ten people born in the Year of the Sheep finds happiness. For this reason, many Chinese parents inquire about early delivery via C-section to ensure a horse-year birth. As a matter of fact, according to Chinese government statistics, January 2015 saw a peek of Caesarean sections, because that was the last month for the year of the horse, and everyone was trying to avoid having unlucky goat babies. However, if you do find yourself with a daughter born in the year of goat, luckily many Chinese also believe that if you have three goats in your family they can apparently eliminate all the bad luck that one goat caused. So just start counting goats or sheep...

Jingjing finally became pregnant and started to plan for the date of the C-section. It just so happened that the due date for what turned out to be a little girl was around September 1. She consulted both a numerologist and a fortune teller to find the best and most auspicious date to bring her daughter into the world.

Many superstitions in China are based on homophones in the language. As Chinese is a tonal language, it follows that many words and otherwise unrelated concepts are pronounced the same or nearly the same way. When these unrelated concepts are treated as if they were related, then over time numerous taboos and superstitious beliefs have developed. This makes certain numbers more auspicious than others. The sixth and eighth days of the lunar month (according to the Chinese lunar calendar–or if that doesn't work then the Gregorian one will have to do the trick), or dates with a six, eight and nine in them, are all popular. The luckiest of them all, however, is eight, or "*ba*" which in the southern Cantonese dialect is pronounced "*baat*". In both cases, this sounds like the word "*fa*" or in Cantonese "*faat*", which can mean "to get rich." On the other hand, no one wants to give birth on a day or a date with four in it. They are avoided at all cost because "four" (*si*) is a close homonym for the word for 'death', also pronounced "*si*", though with a different tone. Accordingly, Tomb Sweeping Day (often April 4th, making it double four, where the Chinese honour their ancestors), is of course shunned by all means. And many buildings in China lack a fourth floor, or even a 14th or a 24th floor if they're tall enough. Some even skip the 13th floor as well–not a Chinese superstition, but better to be safe than sorry! Phone numbers which have a particularly lucky combination of sixes, eights, and nines are auctioned off for thousands, even millions (the number 88888888 was sold for nearly RMB 3 million), while numbers ending in something like '94' can be acquired for almost nothing or even be had for free because *"jiu si"* in Chinese, as well as meaning the numbers nine and four also sounds like the Chinese for either "long and slow death" or "about to die". My company had given me one such phone number... Guess they think that these superstitions don't work on foreigners.

Jingjing also considered her daughter's education. Six years is the minimum age for elementary school entrance in China, so to allow for her daughter to be old enough for the autumn semester when she is six years old, she chose to have the C-section about one week earlier than her original due date. Jingjing had then planned to send the girl to a full time, see-your-child-once-a-month, kindergarten. These are both very numerous and popular around China for working parents who for one reason or the other don't have time for their children. They are generally considered to be a good environment for the child to grow up in, beginning learning early on so the child can be competitive and get ahead in society. But luckily (my opinion entirely), not everything went as planned. Even though she was allowed to pick an auspicious date for the C-section, Jingjing is still married and the little girl is so far attending a pretty normal Chinese kindergarten.

Another Chinese friend, Jiajia, who gave birth to a boy just a few months after Luka was born, found out that both Fu and herself had seen the same obstetrician. She asked Fu how she had chosen the obstetrician, and Fu replied that it was by chance. Jiajia was surprised, to say the least. She explained that she had taken a whole sheet of photographs of all the obstetricians, copy and pasted from the website, and shown it to a fortune teller. He had then chosen the doctor for her just by looking at the shape and expression on their faces. I'm just thinking, what if he had chosen the intern?

Just as I had asked my friends about their experiences in China during their wife's pregnancy, I also asked them when they knew they had become a dad in China. One friend wrote: "When a sheet is placed on top of the baby's head in order to protect it from 'eating cold wind' and it's at least 35 degrees Celsius." My friend Philip said: "When people tell you in all honesty that you should find an old lady who can expel the fear from the baby's body if it has been startled. The fear comes out of the soft spot on top of the head." Jes added: "When I had been away for only a couple of weeks on business and your child has been fully potty trained by your mother-in-law", and added that: "When I dragged my mother-in-law to the car to teach her how to strap in the child's seat in the back and she defiantly refused to participate." And he finished by saying the time he was most embarrassed was when his *ayi* pulled his daughters pants down on a public bus because she has said "she needs a wee" and I stood up to say "no child of mine…"

Hospitals in China are normally catagorized as either a Traditional Chinese Medicine (TCM) hospital or a normal (Western-style medicine) hospital. However, at many normal hospitals, there are also TCM departments, and Chinese doctors also often combine TCM and normal prescription medicine as well as treatments. But asking for TCM treatment at a normal hospital might not get the response you'd expected. I once went with a really bad lower back pain and suggested TCM, and the

Chinese doctor just looked at me and said, "that's not an option". He even laughed at me for asking about acupuncture or massage or a combination. He was sure it was kidney stones and would only give me a lot of pain killers–and an expensive ultrasound.

TCM in China exists in some ways in a kind of black hole between tradition and modernity, but ironically over the last few decades there has been a significant increase in the practice and use of TCM in the West. Many Westerners have come to realize that this ancient practice has its place in modern society, and its most well-known remedy, acupuncture, is used extensively by more and more doctors with good results. In the treatment of illnesses and conditions such as infertility, there are studies which show that acupuncture can increase the chances for a baby by up to 15 percent, and it is used for morning sickness, for the recovery of stroke patients, and as anaesthesia during major operations such as heart surgery (both during and after the operation) and also during childbirth. In one study published in the *American Journal of Obstetrics and Gynecology* in 2004, acupuncture was compared with conventional care. The result was that the women receiving acupuncture during childbirth requested significantly fewer pain-relieving interventions, such as epidural, than the women not receiving acupuncture. And among the same group of women, 86 percent said they would use it again for another childbirth.

TCM has been in existence for over 2,000 years, and has been an integral part of Chinese culture intertwined with both spiritual and religious practice throughout history. I have offered myself over the years as an experimental porcupine and received other TCM treatments as well, including "cupping" several times. This is where numerous glass cups were placed upside down on my back and vacuum suction was created using a flame, resulting in my back looking like I had been locked up in a medieval torture chamber. Most visits actually had very positive effects.

So, being in the land of acupuncture and naïve as I am, I thought it would be natural to ask at the maternity hospital if Fu could have acupuncture during the delivery to ease her pain. The doctor looked at me in disbelief. In fact, not a single one of the Beijing hospitals we visited before we finally chose the private hospital offered acupuncture. I asked around and one doctor told me that, in fact, it had been commonplace to use acupuncture as anaesthesia back in the days before the one child policy was inaugurated. After that, the practice quickly died out. Modern methods have taken over, and, as Fu and her friends have told me, are generally seen as more advanced and safer than acupuncture. And as we have already seen–with the delivery of the one and only child, no one is taking any chances!

An American friend of mine, Josie, who is married to a Chinese Mongolian, and who also happens to be a doctor of TCM, was giving birth at the same private hospital as us. The doctor suggested she should get a C-section as the delivery had already protracted quite a long time, but most importantly because the baby was not upside down as it was supposed to be. Josie refused. Her Chinese husband as well as all the Chinese staff at the hospital were staring at her in disbelief when she then opted to wait for her American friend, also a trained TCM doctor and acupuncturist, to come and treat her to alleviate the pain, and also use moxibustion (a therapy using a dried plant called moxa which is most often burned close to the skin of the acupuncture point next to the fifth toes of both feet) in order to try to turn the baby around.

Josie told me about her experience. "The hospital did not offer acupuncture, and in fact when the baby was on her way out with her bottom first they advised against using moxa to turn her. In fact, there have been several scientific studies done in both Italy,

Spain, China and Switzerland that showed this worked much better than anything else."

Actually, one study involving 1,346 pregnant women showed a 74% decrease in the risk of having a baby come out with the bottom first after using moxa. However, Josie also told me that there were one or two cases in China where they believed it caused the baby to move so that the cord was wrapped around its neck. Josie became very frustrated.

"They are completely risk-adverse here, if there is a *"wanyi"* (literally, one in ten thousand) "what if?" they will not take a chance. It drove me absolutely nuts. Getting prenatal care here was THE most frustrating, irritating experience of my life, and can compete only with the *yuesao* (full time nanny for the first month after delivery) experience in terms of invoking true anger in me."

In the end, Josie got an epidural anyway and with tears in her eyes, also had to agree to a C-section. "My baby was born while a stranger–the anaesthesiologist–held my hand and said, 'the baby is here, I should say congratulations." It was a very anti-climactic delivery for Josie and not what she had wished for at all. Of course, the doctors and staff want to help the patients as much as possible, but the policies are institutional as well as cultural, and unlikely to change in a hurry.

And unlike in the West, nothing seems to indicate that acupuncture is gaining popularity in Chinese maternity hospitals. At the same time, Josie now has an ever increasing number of expat women who come to her Beijing clinic for a series of acupuncture treatments as part of their birth preparation.

After a few months with our new born baby boy, Luka, I, although I was very hard to convince, had to admit that we probably needed a little more space than our cozy courtyard house provided. With Luka in the pram, we travelled around the inner city, slowly expanding the radius as it was very difficult to find something which both fitted our needs and wallet size, looking for a new place to settle. Initially, it was very difficult to move away from both my beloved area around The Forbidden City and the old city center, and also move up in the air. After about two months, looking at at least twenty different places, we finally settled on a fourth floor apartment, twice the size of our former courtyard house, and with a large balcony, just outside the second ring road, and old city wall and gate, Andingmen, 10 kilometres Northeast. Andingmen means the gate of bringing peace. That is also what it did for us, bringing peace to our relationship. Among local old Beijingers, however, the gate used to be known as the gate of excrements. In the past the excrements of the city was collected at certain places just North of the Altar of the Earth, to be made into fertilizer. The wheel barrows and other vehicles carrying the human leftovers from a city of about a million inhabitants, would for hundred of years pass through Andingmen. According to old Beijingers this trade was good business. But the quality of the fertilizer produced would vary according to where the excrements came from. Excrements from the North was more expensive than excrements from the South of the city, simply because the nutrition of the food eaten in the rich North and the poor South was different. After 1949 this practice slowly vanished, but had surely left the earth in the area well fertilized for centuries to come. Our compound was called Lihong Garden, and our balcony overlooked a luxuriant large park like compound dotted with priceless "slip carefully" signs in front of the faux paper mache like rocks, and lined with Chinese temple and fruit trees. However, the grass was still off-limits with signs stating "Lawn no trample". Built in the late 1990s, the *loufang* was no architectural wonder and already somewhat worn down, (the average building in China is built to last about 30 years), but we immediately took to the local feel of the area with its bustling markets, interesting shops, and lively restaurants representing everything you could wish for from all corners of the Chinese culinary spectrum from delicious dim-sum to spicy ducks necks and freshly roasted chestnuts during the winter. They also almost all offered tasty take-away, and even the Chongqing Representative Office's restaurant, serving mouth-watering renderings of pungent and Sichuan pepper soaked Chongqing favorites, was just ten minutes away. So just like in the distant past, we ate well in the North and in turn Luka, who was a little on the skinny side for the first few months, also quickly fattened up (before he was three years old, the doctor told us Luka would grow up to be around two meters (6,6 ft) tall). And still, despite the hustle and bustle of the city just outside, life within the compound nevertheless retained a serene feel to it and we even had a good humored, two sizes too big, but nattily attired guard at our front door. So what's not to like?

10

BLOND OR BLACK?

FU SOMETIMES jokingly says when looking at our two handsome sons. "I only married you to get beautiful children". And while I certainly hope that's not that case, if she had wanted them to be blond and blue-eyed like David Bowie promised his *China Girl* when he sang "I'll give you eyes of blue", we did not succeed. And actually this is not so surprising.

If you are reading this, chances are you are a human, in which case you probably have 46 chromosomes (23 pairs). If you were a panda you would have 42, and if you were a mosquito you would have to live with only 6 chromosomes. Chromosomes are the genetic material that makes up a living creature. Each of your parents contributed half of your genetic material, and most of the time, of course, that means your children will look a little bit like both you and your partner. But this is not always the case.

A god-fearing white American couple from Arkansas, USA, got quite a surprise when the mother miraculously delivered a black baby. The parents of the little boy were stunned. "We are sure it's our kid, but we don't know why he looks black." Conversely, a black British couple gave birth to a white baby girl, with the stunned dad declaring, "I'm sure she's my kid, I just don't know why she's blond." Similarly, a French-Chinese couple in our compound had a completely blond child, so blond that the Chinese mother might have started wondering herself. I actually took the mother for the babysitter when we first met.

"*Dou shi wo de cuo*", meaning "It's all my fault", are the lyrics of a little song that my Danish friend who became a dad the day before me, always sings. It's the heavy burden of being a father, and maybe just a little more if your partner is Chinese. You try winning an argument on cultural matters with someone from a culture that claims five, six or even seven thousands years of history (why is it that number always seems to go up but not down?).

Expect to be blamed for just about everything that is wrong, or wrong in your wife's eyes, with your baby. First of all, chances are that he or she was difficult to push out in the first place. Your foreign gene pool has made the baby quite a lot bigger than the average Chinese baby. Both of mine have been both on the long and heavy side, and since I have experienced both deliveries at the side of my wife while feeling helpless when she was in excruciating pain, I thank God that he made the woman give birth and not the man! Dear female readers and mothers: We feel for you and with you, but we will never, ever understand completely what you are going through. "It's all your fault! Your foreign gene pool and Viking ancestors." I happily take all the blame so long as I don't have to go through a delivery myself.

In our compound lived a couple, a stocky American father and small petite Chinese mother, who had possibly the biggest, fattest baby I have ever seen. Poor guy-he has probably born the blame for this many times. And of course, poor girl too. That goes without saying.

Genes determine, among other things, skin color, the size of the eyes, number of fingers and toes, and hair color, and they are either 'recessive' or 'dominant'. These two different kinds of genes are called alleles.

BLOND OR BLACK?

To make a long, complicated story short, the allele for dark hair is dominant over the allele for blond hair (the same goes for brown eyes over blue, green and grey eyes), and that means that even if you are the blondest of Scandinavians, there is only a 25 percent chance your child will have blonde hair. These are the odds every time you have a child. And despite the fact the odds are quite low, you can at least theoretically have four blonde and blue-eyed children even with a Chinese spouse.

Let me give you another slightly less savoury example. The allele for dry earwax originated by mutation in northeast Asia about 2,000 generations ago and has frequencies close to 100 percent in people from northern China and Korea, but it is uncommon in Europe, and almost completely absent in Africa. The allele for wet earwax is dominant over the allele for dry earwax, so both our sons now have the unfavourable wet earwax. In China, true or not, wet earwax is also associated with sweating more and emitting greater body odour. Here I have to admit one thing: Compared to the average Chinese, Westerners, (including myself), sweat like sinners in church. At least you now know there's not much you can do about it.

However lovely babies look when cute and small, appearances can easily change. For better or for worse, depending on your view. I was as blond as Legolas from *The Lord of the Rings* as a child, but later my hair turned a rather boring shade of liver pâté. For a long time, Louis, our number two son, sort of had one Chinese eye and one Western eye, but they later balanced off with the same size. His eyelashes started short and then grew much longer. And the golden blond French-Chinese child in our compound probably ended up with brown hair.

Fortunately, the Chinese generally strongly believe that children of mixed Asian-Western couples are very beautiful, and if you are lucky, some of your genes will have contributed to that. Several of the traits considered especially beautiful by the Chinese, and which many Westerners have, include large eyes, long eyelashes, and a Roman nose (other traits considered especially attractive include pale-white skin, and, particularly for women, a face shaped like a goose egg or a melon seed), and they are all dominant genes. The Chinese actually believe that a person's nose (actually its size, no matter how out of place it may look!) is the best measure of a person's potential to get rich. In Chinese face-reading, the nose is known as the 'prosperity palace' and men who possess a fleshy nose are very popular and sought-after by old aunts and grandmothers scouting for potential sons-in-law. Unfortunately, some of the less attractive genes for i.e. my baldness, are also dominant.

With China being very much a 'survival of the fittest' sort of country, with all members of the huge Chinese population fighting for pretty much everything–health care, education, jobs, resources and even spouses–genes matter quite a lot. On top of that, if you consider that most couples will only have one child, they become even more important.

The Maternal and Infant Health Law passed in 1995 and aimed at restricting births believed to be imperfect, actually suggests that in order to prevent 'inferior births', those 'deemed unsuitable for reproduction' should undergo sterilization or abortion or be compelled to remain celibate. I know of several examples where either the young Chinese woman or man have chosen to end a relationship, even if they already had decided to get married, because their partner was found to have a bad "gene"–even one related to a very common condition such as hypertension.

11

WHAT'S IN A NAME?

IN CHINA, quite a lot actually. Choosing the name of our first child was more complicated than we could have ever imagined. And as most of our Chinese friends and acquaintances have consulted a fortune teller, and even if they haven't directly chosen a name on his recommendation, they have at least consulted him on the name they were thinking about giving the new born baby, we could not deviate from this. For babies with Chinese mothers and foreign fathers (or the other way around), I think in most cases they will be given both a Chinese and a foreign name. Mine did.

Chinese names always carry a meaning and its most often something good and pleasant. Girl's names normally relates to beauty, flowers, scent or pureness. Boys names are usually connected with power, bravery or wealth. Some of the most common boy's names in China are *Wei*, meaning 'great', *Qiang* meaning 'strong', and *Jun* meaning 'army', so we wanted to avoid those. But first we would have to settle on the last name.

All foreigners in China will at some point get a made-up Chinese name. It could be arbitrarily chosen by a Chinese friend or teacher and is usually based on similar sounds or sometimes the direct meaning of the foreign name. Mine is *Ge Ximeng*. It was chosen by my first Chinese teacher in Chengdu, Liu *Laoshi*, and is based on the sounds. As it would be ridiculous to use my "invented" Chinese last name for the boys, they got my wife's last name, *Deng*, as in Deng Xiaoping (no relation as far as we know). In this type of situation, some Chinese in-laws, however, are afraid of the loss of face they will occur on account of their grandchildren having the same last name as the mother, because it can suggest that their daughter has had illegitimate children.

Delving a little into Fu's family history, however, revealed a very interesting story. Fu's grandfather, who was a famous children's doctor of traditional Chinese medicine, was adopted into the Deng family, when his parents gave him up to their best friends. Whereas the Yang family had plenty of sons, the Deng family had none, so an agreement was made that the young boy *Shaoxian* would simply change address and family name. So Fu's actual ancestors are within the *Yang* family clan, and as such they believe to be descendants of the Qiang people, a Central Asian nomadic tribe still inhabiting areas of northwestern Sichuan. This could maybe help to explain some of Fu's family members with curly hair and warrior like built.

Regardless, Luka became Deng Lujia (where '*jia*'-珈 is a kind of precious jade that women wore on the top of their head in ancient times), and Louis became Deng Luyi (signifying that he should both be able to be hard working, but also know when to relax, because the character for 'yi' (驛) means a resting place, or a place for changing horses), but not before my wife had consulted her sister-in-law who has a thing or two up her sleeve when it comes to fortune-telling and Chinese folk beliefs, and she helped us by searching through all her literature on the subject. Sharing the same character *Lu* (路, literally meaning "road" or "to walk"), in addition to sharing the surname *Deng*, was an attempt at creating a traditional Chinese generation name (*zibei*) for them. This is a name given to the descendants by the ancestors

WHAT'S IN A NAME?

of the family usually with implications of auspiciousness and prosperity. And as generation names have traditionally mostly been used for boys, it was only fitting. "When in China...".

It may sound like it was a relatively simple process to choose their names. However, it was actually not that easy to find a proper name that we could agree on. To begin with, Fu is from Sichuan, and the dialect there, as with most Chinese dialects in southern and southwest China, encounters some variations with the letters "l", "n", and "r" depending on the position in the word and the letter that comes after. This meant that quite a lot of names weren't feasible from the beginning. Anything with "le", "la", "ne", "na", "re", and "ra" were simply out of the question. And as many Danish and Scandinavian names have plenty of these, we would have to venture out a bit further beyond the cold Nordic Viking waters.

Another thing about many Western names are that they are simply too long and difficult to pronounce for most Chinese. And even names that we think are relatively short can still become quite long in Chinese. Take the king himself, Elvis Presley. In Chinese he becomes "*Ai'er wei si Pu la si li*"–(I have separated the pinyin into its component characters so you can see just what a mouthful it is!). Many names end with an 's', just like Elvis, which is a problem, as then it comes out as '*si*', which sounds like "death" in Chinese. Not a good start. Just consider what happened to Elvis! (In the 1950s, when Elvis rose to global stardom, the Chinese outside of mainland China solved this problem by naming him *Maowang*–Cat King.)

There was yet another obstacle. Because in the Sichuan dialect 'hu' becomes '*fu*', so "*huzhao*" (passport) becomes "*fuzhao*" and "*laohu*" (tiger) turns into "*laofu*", then yet more options disappeared.

Starting from scratch and a few lists of possible names, we both started to underline boys names that we liked.

There is actually a Chinese saying about how important a good name is: *ci zi qian jin, bu ru jiao zi yi yi. Jiao zi yi yi, bu ru ci zi hao ming.* Translated it means something like: Instead of giving your child gold, teach him a skill; instead of teaching him a skill, give him a good name." So we worked quite hard to find the perfect name.

Finally, we decided on "Luka" as his non-Chinese name. The name came to me one day when I went out for lunch in Beijing's Sanlitun shopping area to a Vietnamese / Mexican restaurant called Luga's (they make a darn good chicken burrito and pho noodle soup). I have also always really liked the song by Suzanne Vega, *My name is Luka,* although it wasn't until we fixed on that name that I realized the lyrics are actually about child abuse! Maybe subconsciously it was the many years spent in Chinese markets, where the Chinese sellers continuously chant at foreigners "Look'a! Look'a!" Whatever the real reason, thankfully Fu liked the name too. We purposely chose not to add the 's' at the end, both because so many kids seemed to be named Lukas or Lucas, and because of the above mentioned 's' = death problem. For the same reason, Louis has a silent 's', just as the French say it.

Contrary to all Chinese common sense, we chose the name "Luka" a couple of months before he was born. Customarily Chinese people would not even dream about settling on a name before the child comes into this world because it brings misfortune.

In the past, it was not uncommon for Chinese girls, especially from poorer families, to have no name at all. Fu's grandfather actually had to find a name for his wife, as she had none. At the same time, however, especially for boys of a wealthy or cultured

WHAT'S IN A NAME?

background, it was common to have a whole array of names during a lifetime. But Chinese kids today have an official name which parents need to choose within a month, and also usually a "milk name", a "*ruming*" or a "*xiaoming*", typically employing doubled characters, often, but not always, the last character in their given name, before a formal name is settled upon.

In the countryside, names such as "*Gougou*" (dog) and "*Niuniu*" (cow) are popular because these animals are easy to raise. In our compound, we have quite a few "*Niunius*", but we also have a little girl named "*Ji Dezhu*" which means "to remember", a boy named "*Zhenshuai*", meaning "really good looking" and another little girl named "*Zhu Baoshi*" which translates as "jewelry". We even have a set of twins called "*Pingping*" and "*An'an*", capitalizing on the word "*Ping'an*", meaning "peaceful". Similarly a set of sisters named *Wang Mei* and *Wang Li*, combining to create the word "*Meili*", meaning beautiful. I have given up on keeping track of who goes by their real name and who goes by their milk name. A superstitious custom sometimes attached to the milk name is to select a disgusting name, or give a small boy a girl's name, in order to ward off evil spirits who might wish to harm the child or even kidnap him or her during early childhood. If this was not enough, many Chinese people also get a school name, *xueming*, used only while in school, a calling name, used by friends and family, and a style, pen or courtesy name, originally given to males when they reached maturity and most often used on formal occasions. My father-in-law actually used a pen-name for many years. It was: Deng Ye. "*Ye*" meaning "sparkling bright".

To choose the most auspicious name, usually both the grandparents and a fortune teller are consulted. The day and exact time of the delivery are needed for the fortune teller (part of the reason why C-sections are so popular in China). He or she uses the 'five elements' (wood, metal, water, fire, and earth) of which missing elements can be added to the characters chosen to achieve balance, and also both the theory of Yin and Yang and the 12 Chinese zodiac animals, with the correct number of strokes in the Chinese character, all to determine the best possible name for the child. The milk name may be abandoned but is often continued as a nickname.

Apart from *meimei* (little sister), and *Fu'er*, her nick name, *hao*, Fu's parents mostly call her by her full name, Deng Fu. Every time they do it, I just can't help myself thinking "oh no", now she will be scolded–"Deng Fu, go and clean your room", or "Deng Fu, finish your dinner", but luckily it is nothing of the sort.

For a selected few, mostly royalty, there were even more names: a reign name, a temple name, used on the ancestral tablets worshipped by younger generations, and to top it up a posthumous honorary name. The infamous Empress Dowager Cixi ended up with what must be the longest posthumous name ever created: "The Empress who is Admirably Filial, Initiates Kindness, with Blessed Health, Manifests Much Contentment, Solemn Sincerity, with Longevity, Provides Admiration Prosperously, Reveals Adoration, Prosperous with a Merry Heaven, with a Holy Appearance".

Children are rarely named after historical figures or ancestors, and being named after a parent is still quite uncommon. Instead Chinese babies are often named after significant events, such as when children born during a 7.0 magnitude earthquake that hit Lijiang in China's south-western Yunnan province in 1996, were named *"Zhensheng,"* meaning "born from a quake." Or when more than 4,000 children in China were named *"Aoyun"*, meaning "Olympic Games", in the years leading up to the Beijing Olympics in 2008 (actually the name Olympia was rather common in the west in the early twentieth century). The official

WHAT'S IN A NAME?

mascots of the Beijing Games were the "Five Friendlies"–*Bei Bei, Jing Jing, Huan Huan, Ying Ying and Ni Ni*. So in addition to the 4,000 plus *Aoyuns*, another 4,000 or so children received the name of one of these mascots. In another case, 14 babies in China were named "Chang'e, in honor of China's first lunar satellite which was launched in late 2007. If you are completely out of ideas and the opportunity arises you ask a famous person to pick the name. Such an opportunity came for Facebook founder, Marc Zuckerberg and his pregnant American-Chinese wife Priscilla Chan, at a White House state dinner in Xi Jinping's honor in 2015. Zuckerberg simply plucked up the courage and asked Xi to name their unborn daughter in Mandarin. Xi, however, returned the request with a stony-face and a definitive 'no'.

Another Chinese tradition is to augment a name by adding the historical name of the city or province you were born in. As it happens, this is the same name as is now used to denote said region on license plates. To give you an example you would say "*Shu*" for Sichuan province or its provincial capital Chengdu, "*Yu*" for Chongqing, the megacity on the Yangtze River, "*Hu*" for Shanghai and "*Jing*" for the capital Beijing. As an example, Wu Jing, the well-known Chinese martial artist, actor and director, is from Beijing.

It is also very popular to name your child after successful film and sports stars. At least 5,000 children have been named after Yao Ming, the 2.29 meter-tall former Houston Rockets basketball star.

Some parents even choose names which touch on social themes. Words such as "responsibility" (*Zeren*), and "harmonious" (*Hexie*) are popular because they were the Hu Jintao / Wen Jiabao administration buzz word of the 2000s. "Harmonious society" (*hexie shehui*) was an oft-used phrase on public notices and elsewhere. Also, more than 6,600 Chinese are named "democracy" (*Minzhu*). Countless Chinese children have been named *"Wenming"*, meaning civilization. This is probably a result of the endless number of civilization / civilizing campaigns carried out in China's cities in the last decade, the government hoping the conduct of its citizens could match the government's own aspirations as an emerging superpower.

The "people" of China are commonly called the *laobaixing*, which literally translates as the "old hundred surnames". About forty percent of all these *laobaixing* share one of the top ten most popular last names like Wang, Li and Zhang. Little wonder that there's a strong drive for individuality with given names! A lot of parents say they want their children to be unique. In fact, it seems to be a worldwide trend. In my opinion, not always in the best interests of the children who might well hate you for it later on.

For a number of years this meant that Chinese parents started using less common characters, numbers and symbols and even letters borrowed from other alphabets, but this has now been banned. One such innovation was the @ sign–which, when pronounced with a drawn out "T" sounds like "*Aita*", and translates to "love him / her". I'm guessing the parents, who by the way were not permitted to use this name in the end, met via online dating.

In China, the surname normally comes from the father, but it can be taken from either side, and some Chinese couples even try to do what is very common in the West–namely to combine the two last names.

Many countries put a number of restrictions on names. China has now joined in. Only Chinese characters are permitted; however, if the name is deemed a swearword, seen as anti-China or anti-party, or contains characters which are unable to be

WHAT'S IN A NAME?

inputted on computers and thus in the public databases, then they are also prohibited. A typical Chinese name normally constitutes two or three characters, four characters are occasionally seen—two-character surnames — and any more than that is very rare. Citizens belonging to ethnic minority groups such as Mongols, Tibetans and Uighurs, however, often have many syllables when their names are written in Chinese.

There are more than 50,000 Chinese characters, yet only about half of these are supported by computer software. This means that around 60 million Chinese face the problem that their names use old characters so obscure that computers cannot recognize them. Even if you are head of state and have imperial ancestry, this can be difficult to overcome. Former Premier and distant relative of the founder of the Ming dynasty, Zhu Rongji has this problem. His name has a rare "*rong*" character that still gives the Chinese media headaches. Whether anyone of these 60 million people like it or not, because of the limits of the digital reality we live in, they simply have to get used to another name–not the pronunciation, but the Chinese character with which it is written.

Money is the mantra of modern China. "Money" (*qian*) is even a last name here. I read one day in the Chinese parenting magazine *Fumu* (Parents) how a couple had chosen the name Qian Duoduo for their son. It would translate as "Money More More". I also have a Chinese friend called "Youqian", which means "have money" (which he has always claimed is very far from the truth!). The Hong Kong-based Phoenix TV once made a show where Chinese children had to answer a number of questions, such as "what is happiness?", as well as having to explain what their parents talked about. The majority of the children answered that all their parents were talking about was money.

On one hand, a new trend in China is that parents born in

the 1980s and after, now often name their children after famous figures in popular computer games. On the other hand, money or computer-game-related names might be more suitable for the present generation than the millions who grew up with political and militaristic names such as "the East is Red", "Red Army", "Five Stars" (after the national flag) "Founding of the Nation", or siblings named "Leap" and "Forward" after the Great Leap Forward campaign in 1958-61 which ironically turned out to be a Great Leap Backward and disastrously killed around 30-50 million Chinese. One such famous family, is the Ling family of four brothers and one sister who have all fallen from communist political stardom on corruption charges after Xi Jinping took power in 2013. All siblings were named after Mao-era Communist Party terminology. I.e. *Ling Jihua*, whose name means "planning" was chief of the General Office of the Communist Party from 2007-2012, and whose son was famously killed in a black Ferrari car accident after racing on the ring roads of Beijing during the midnight hours.

These names were especially popular in the countryside for children born through the 1950-70s, which means that many former peasants, who are now living in the cities, have wanted to change their names to something sounding less stereotypically farmer-like.

So that's Chinese names. But what about the English / foreign names that Chinese people give themselves? Increasingly, more and more Chinese parents choose to give their child an English name to begin with. Angela, Henry, Lucy, John and Cindy have all become quite common, although they still have to retain a Chinese name for official documents. However, I find many Chinese come up with funny or strange English names for themselves when they go abroad or when working with

WHAT'S IN A NAME?

foreigners in China. It is quite often because foreigners cannot pronounce their names properly (real or imagined), like my former colleague who named all his (unlucky) students after his favourite country & western singers. The school had a whole class of Midwestern stars: Dolly, Patty, Kenny, Billy-Ray, Bobby, Hank, Willie, Garth etc. Often they seem to make names up, like Tear, Fish and Fire, some even sounding lethal like Urania (from Greek mythology I suppose) or it could just be a direct translation of their Chinese name, such as Gold and Silver. Sometimes it sounds like a weather forecast with lots of people choosing the names Sunny, Rain, Fog and even Flood, topped up with the four seasons. At times it's difficult to take the names seriously. I met a forty-year-old man named Rainbow, another who called himself Linda, and a waitress in a coffee shop had "Darcy" on her name tag. There are numerous people called Happy, Sugar, Candy, and even Kinky and I once met a Cinderella (none of these were strippers or prostitutes).

I've met whole fruit baskets of people: Orange, Apple, Lemon, Mango and even a Cucumber and Potato thrown in. Who said the Chinese are not innovative? I had a student named Shredder (not sure if it was because he loved (or hated) the Ninja Turtles), one called Lucifer (maybe he really was a Satanist), and another one who insisted on being called "Michael Jackson".

Equally, foreigners in China also often end up with funny names. This does not, however, include my own. My own name, *Ge Ximeng*, is a combination of a last name of a famous Chinese actor called *Ge You* (which sounds a bit like my own last name, but have made quite a number of restaurant waiters completely baffled on the phone when they mistakenly think that the famous actor will come to their restaurant). The sound of my first name in Chinese literally means "Western Mongol", which to a Westerner sounds funny, but is a common transliteration of 'Simon'. Luckily others amply make up for it. One of the most common Chinese name for foreign males include the ubiquitous *Da Long*, meaning "Big Dragon", which seems to insinuate something more down there. Another funny or strange idea is to use names of famous historical figures, like my friend who took the name *Wu Sangui*, the name of a Ming dynasty general who gave up the defence of Beijing and ran away to far-off southwestern China. "Why?" I asked. "Because then people will remember me." And he was right, people do remember!

In fact, it doesn't matter what name your child ends up with or whether they love you or hate you for it, because in China like in many other countries, it is always possible to change your name. But most people don't go through the hassle to change the name on official documents; it is only for their everyday use, even though this can be rather confusing. The Chinese equivalent of the numerologist–the fortune-teller–does good business these days, and I personally know three Chinese who changed their name in order to change their fate. Whether or not it actually worked, I am not sure. I will have to ask them. But of course, how would they ever really know?

12

RE-EDUCATION THROUGH LABOUR

ARRIVING HOME where summer had turned to winter in just a week, covering our courtyard in central Beijing with a thick layer of dirty, grey snow, I was pretty confident that having survived nine months of pregnancy and its accompanying age-old Chinese beliefs, we would now quickly and naturally fall into the roles of being new parents and we could just relax. Boy, was I wrong!

Even though the Chinese system of 're-education through labour'–known as *laojiao*, is part of China's criminal justice system which normally includes some form of political education–is officially on its way out, after being used since the mid-1950s, I quickly realized that in some ways it still existed, as there were still many things (read: superstitions and taboos) I did not know about and even less how to handle. I got to learn about them the hard way.

In China, it is normal that the grandmother on either side, or sometimes both sides, moves in straight after the baby is home and then continues to stay on for the next year or so. Or maybe they won't ever leave again. Oh my god, was my first thought. Both my mother and father-in-law came to stay two weeks after Luka was born and I'll readily admit that they were both a great help during that time, and why wouldn't they be? I actually also had to travel out of town for work so it was perfect for us.

"Happy Mother-in-law, Pretty Daughter-in-law" is the name of a popular Chinese TV-comedy drama series, and even though I would have to change the last part to "Pretty Wife", I'd still like to have a happy mother-in-law. That being said, we did not agree on all of my *yuemu's* (mother-in-law) and *yuefu's* (father-in-law) suggestions, such as Fu not showering or washing her hair for a month, or the rice pillow for Luka so he could get a beautiful flat head, or the amount of soup made on pig trotters Fu had to slurp down. (She confided to me that she had eaten enough pig trotters to last for the rest of her lifetime).

Before the delivery, we agreed that Fu should just eat a varied and healthy diet after giving birth, and that I would be cooking some good food to get her back in shape as quickly as possible. After we got back home, however, we felt a great pressure on our young parenting shoulders.

How could we, in good conscience, opt out a five-six-or maybe even seven (does it ever stop?) thousand year old Chinese tradition for what you should eat and drink as a breast feeding mother, my father-in-law asked me. From day one, my in-laws called every day from morning till evening, asking what Fu had been eating and drinking at her last meal. A ritual I had to learn to live with.

"Oh no!", was my spontaneous reply when I heard Fu repeating what she was being told on the phone. It was a call from a good friend who told Fu that the *yuezi* had gone well, and explaining that his wife hadn't showered, had not left the room, and hadn't even opened the window for a whole month after giving birth to a healthy boy. The *yuezi* or actually the *zuo yuezi* he was talking about, literally means "sitting for a month".

With these Chinese friends I just had not seen it coming, I guess. He had been living in Germany for many years and the fact that she was a former model, would kind of prevent them from going through this whole thing. At least that is what I expected.

But the fact is that the majority of Chinese women "sit for a month" after giving birth. It is also called confinement, which probably to many Western ears sound like something out of a Victorian novel. In reality that means that they will stay at home with the baby for the first month, or in Beijing–exactly 42 days (which was the day when the boys had their first check-up after being born). Some will literally sit or rather lie down on the bed the whole time. We joked quite a lot about that before the delivery. Could that really be necessary? "Old superstition," I said. " I have friends who have climbed The Great Wall and been water skiing less than two weeks after the delivery," I continued.

Even though Fu did not stay at home all 42 days, I have to admit, that it actually does make sense; because she was in fact quite weak after having given birth. However, it was still a little bit strange that our Chinese relatives and friends did not come visiting during the first weeks. But as I learned, the intention was to spare the mother and son, and so it was absolutely normal that they waited to come and offer congratulations after the first month had passed. Only after the mother had fully recovered and Luka had matured slightly was it time to celebrate. Many elderly Chinese women relate their ailments like headaches, arthritis, and intestinal gas among others to not having fully observed rules, written as well unwritten, during their *yuezi*.

As described above, according to Chinese custom, the woman cannot bathe or wash her hair for the first month. Some even go as far as to not brush their teeth! But that's where I put my foot down. Before running hot water, it made sense, but in the twenty-first century? Luckily we did not have to debate that one, even though both our neighbour and my mother-in-law put pressure on Fu to do the opposite. Mrs Li, next door advised Fu not to watch any sad movies that could make her cry as the mood affects the liver and can also cause eye disease. As a matter of fact, Fu was told, she should not read, watch TV or DVDs, send or receive text messages, make or take calls on her phone or play on her tablet or computer as any straining of the eyes was potentially bad. However, Mrs Li added, "It's okay to listen to the radio." She also warned Fu that "if you take a shower, your body will take in too much water and then you will become damp and get a cold." Wonderful!

But as one new Chinese mother found out, too warm can also be a serious problem. It made major headlines in the Chinese media and created quite some debate online when a Chinese mother sadly died of heatstroke following advice from her family to cover up during her *yuezi* period. The Shanghai woman stayed in a room without any air-conditioning and covered herself with a quilt even when daytime temperatures went above 35 degrees Celsius to avoid the malicious influence of "wind chills", which is considered the major cause of illness in traditional Chinese medicine.

The same goes for the baby. By way of example, my British friend Tom, told me a story of his brother who recently had a son. His wife was in hospital in central London and two midwifes were working on the ward the night after she had her baby. One was Asian, most probably Chinese, the other African from the Caribbean. When the Asian nurse came in, she made sure the newborn baby was bundled tightly in as much clothes and blankets as possible. Later, when the Caribbean nurse passed by, she freaked out and took all the clothes and blankets off. Then the Asian nurse would pass by again and bundle the baby back up, and so on and so on... You get the picture!

Strongly against the advice of pretty much everyone, we

made it out the door about three weeks after both Luka and Louis were born. With Louis in his stroller happily asleep, we sneaked out the door for a walk in our neighbourhood. As all the other women, it seems, in our whole compound knew exactly when Fu had given birth (word spreads quickly), they also knew that she was leaving the house much too early. Every single one we met, looked at her with sincere concern, and after she responded that it was already three weeks, they replied, "ONLY three weeks" and rolled their eyes and looking at me like it was all my fault. But when they heard that we were heading to Starbucks for a cup of coffee, the look on their faces changed and they said: "Coffee!!!????" while they seemed to be thinking, nearly out loud, "Are you mad?" and walked away in disbelief. This is what happens if you marry a foreigner...

I know many people, Chinese as well as local foreigners, who outright lied when they were asked by concerned Chinese neighbors and acquaintances about the date they had delivered the baby, because they had dared to go outside the door before the magic date was up. A German friend told me she was 'caught' this way, with her wet hair sticking out from underneath her hat, God forbid it. And it does not make a difference even if it is forty degrees outside.

After Luka was born, we discovered that it would probably be too "risky" if only I did the cooking. To be on the safe side, Fu downloaded an "after-delivery-menu", that told her exactly what she should eat and drink for a whole month. An arsenal of traditional Chinese herbs now took over the kitchen until all the drawers were bursting, and I had to pass on my 'chef's hat' to our cleaning lady, now promoted to nanny and cook, the talkative and lovely *Xiao Du ayi*, who was just always in a good mood, and who together with most of her family from a small village in Anhui Province, was also the local proprietor of the kiosk, the *xiaomaibu*, managing the whole areas delivery of drinking water and most of the recycling too. She also knew everything about everyone because she managed a little phone booth from where the locals made cheap long-distance calls. Usually Chinese people go by the saying that "in the morning, you should eat like an emperor, during lunch you should eat like a commoner, and for dinner you should eat like a beggar". But during Fu's *yuezi* period, she should of course eat like an emperor, or rather empress, the whole time. And *Xiao Du ayi* did everything she possible could to fulfil that.

I was previously always under the impression that fruit was healthy and full of vitamins but, boy, was I wrong on that one. According to Chinese theories on the *yin* and *yang* of food, most fruit is considered "cold" and thus not good for your health just after giving birth. *Xiao Du ayi's* well-meaning idea to put the fruit on the radiator before Fu ate it, did not work either. The fruit was still "cold" even if it was actually quite hot. One of Fu's friends, whose family comes from southeast China's Fujian province, told her that no woman who had just given birth would be allowed to even drink water or eat any "cold" food for a very long time.

Boiled pig trotters, black skinned chicken, papaya, deer antlers, goose eggs, and fish soup with roe, rice wine, wolfberries, red dates, black fungus, and all kinds of tree bark, roots, leaves (and if you are really hungry–a placenta), on the other hand, are all fine and will improve the flow of the milk, dispel "wind", purify the blood and cleanse the arteries, help get her back in to shape, enhance blood circulation and boost the *yang qi* (life energy) in the body that had been compromised by the delivery.

However, all the exotic ingredients on the menu were not the worst part. Worse yet, was that the usually delicious spicy Sichuan food (from Fu's home province in Southwest China)

RE-EDUCATION THROUGH LABOUR

was turned in to a rather bland experience. Because without Sichuan pepper, soya, salt, vinegar, garlic, anise, and all the other wonderful spices, which had been banned from the wok, it was now a little like sticking your tongue out the window and swallowing. At least on a clear blue-sky Beijing day. I wouldn't try it any other day.

Many families, Chinese as well as foreigners, have an *ayi* to take care of their homes, children and pets. *Ayi* actually means "aunt", but it refers to a maid, nanny or housekeeper. They are mostly women from the countryside who find work in the cities, although it is getting more and more popular to find a foreign *ayi*, i.e. from the Philippines or even an *au pair* from a Western country. We have had some wonderful *ayis*, although it was difficult to compete in uniquenesss, with the one in our compound who announced that she had eaten human flesh back during the hunger years of the Great Leap Forward, around 1958-61. Imagine the stories she could tell your children.

In the very beginning, I did not feel comfortable with an *ayi* and always cleaned up everything before she arrived. It was simply uncomfortable having someone seeing my mess and cleaning it up. Somehow there was a vague feeling of imperialistic guilt. I know many who still feel that way. But like many other foreigners (for many of whom "*ayi*" is one of their first Chinese words), I got over it and it did not take that long. An *ayi* can be many things, a live in maid, or just come around once a week or anything in between. She will clean your house, babysit your children, wash your clothes, maybe cook or even bake your favourite pecan pie to perfection, and do any other chores you need. Some of them even come with a long list of impressive references. So what is not to like and why would anyone need more? This is also what I thought until I heard of the *yuesao*.

Does a woman walking around in your home wearing only pink pyjamas (not exactly a Victoria Secret's model, but pyjamas nonetheless) and intimately giving your wife's breasts a massage every day for 26 days in a row, sound a little kinky and nearly too good to be true? Well then, nevertheless, it is the truth. Welcome to the world of the *yuesao*.

During the second pregnancy, my parents-in-law generously told us they would pay for a *yuesao* (literally "month sister-in-law") for Fu to relieve not only her, but also me, and to help Fu recover quicker than when our first boy Luka was born. We discussed it for a little while and then happily accepted the gift. At the time, it was around 6,000 yuan or a thousand dollars and a lot of money for us. It was, however, an experience with both pros and cons.

Apart from the breast massages (apparently helping to produce more milk) which I have to admit are less kinky than they sound like, the duties of our *yuesao* included changing the diaper and bathing Louis, administering night feeds, checking on Fu's post-natal progress and making special nourishing foods and soups to strengthen her and promote her milk supply. Mussolini would have been proud. The *yuesao* was supposed to run a tight ship, to have everything planned running like clockwork, and keeping the same schedule as Louis, sleeping when he did and caring for him when he was awake. This was at least what it said on the check sheet we had received from the *yuesao* agency. In reality, unsurprisingly she had a hard time keeping up with our new-born. As it happens, the first *yuesao* we had quit after a week, which of course did not exactly help Fu's recovery or peace of mind, because she thought we expected too much from her. Maybe we did, or maybe it was actually because she literally came straight from another job, and had had no time at all to recuperate. It really is a tough job.

RE-EDUCATION THROUGH LABOUR

That being said, having the *yuesao* during the night helped us (mostly me as she would often wake up Fu anyway) to get a decent night's sleep. As I did not have any leave at all after Louis was born, this was a great benefit.

The sleep part was a significant advantage of having a *yuesao*, but even though Fu is Chinese, and thus this should eliminate at least the majority of cultural difficulties, there were also many incidents where it was really difficult to have someone in our home 24-7–of course with the best of intentions–knowing better and telling Fu what she should and should not do. We had, after all, been there and done it all once before.

The costs of a *yuesao*, and an *ayi* for that matter, goes up by 20-30 percent every year and even took an extra jump the year Louis was born because it was the year of the dragon (2012), and millions of Chinese deliberately had waited to give birth during that year partly because of the popular belief that "we are the descendants of the dragon", and simply because the dragon is a symbol of good fortune and sign of intense power. The birth rate in 2012 increased by five percent, resulting in an extra one million babies being born that year in China. Adding to the Chinese preference for "dragon boys", the boy-girl ratio for 2012 was an astonishing 120 to 100.

Only a few years later, an experienced *yuesao* charged as much 20,000 yuan or more than $3,000 a month. It has indeed become a very well-paid job and they are booked months ahead. If you have the checkbook for it, you can even extend this wonderland to a five-star *yuezi* or *yuesao* hotel with 26 days of service and medical staff only a ring-of-the-bell away. It will probably soothe many, especially first-time parents, but will also relieve your wallet of yet another 50-150.000 yuan ($8-25,000). One of our wealthy Chinese friends who was three months pregnant had already booked the *yuesao* hotel. We later heard from other friends that one of the unfortunate outcomes of a stay in the *yuesao* hotel was that the staff was so eager to prove their worth, that since they had taken care of and carried the baby around most of the time, believing that it would give the mother more time to rest, that when they finally checked out, the mother and baby had become near strangers.

My mother-in-law looked at the round back head of our youngest son, Louis, when she saw him for the first time, and announced that it was too bad we had not been paying attention when he was sleeping so he could get a beautiful flat back head. Fu told me later and the next time we were visiting I couldn't help teasing her by asking if she didn't just think that Louis had the most beautiful shaped round head... she did not know exactly what to answer. Back home in Beijing again, Fu met an elderly lady in our compound who told Fu straight to her face that it was a shame that she hadn't gotten the head right. Louis' head was round. Near disaster...

Look around you (but please try to be discreet). It's true. Many Chinese have a completely flat back head. What is it with that? Do they all want to look like Bart Simpson?

According to tradition, a flat back head together with a wide forehead symbolizes wealth and honor. And if it comes together with big ears and earlobes, you can add longevity to the lucky bunch. Apparently the tradition goes back to the Qing Dynasty (1644-1911), where the ruling Manchus considered a flat back head to be beautiful. They would tie down the children on the bed so they would not be able to move around by themselves and they would have the babies sleep on a pillow full of either rice or husked sorghum inside. After some time, the baby's back head would become more and more flat. The Manchus even had a saying about this, sounding something like this: "If you sleep well on your back head you will help your forehead become successful". And another slightly simpler old saying goes:

"*qian tu jin, hou tu yin*" meaning that a wide forehead is gold while a protruding back head is only silver.

So the Chinese took over this custom like many others from the Manchus, and today it is still a sign of beauty if the back of the head is flat. And like in the old days, millions of parents around China who strive to acquire this beautiful shape will often put rice into the baby's pillow. Sometimes a book is even tied around the back of the baby's head.

As I mentioned above, the ears are also important. In the West, a big-eared person is not considered to be attractive or lucky; but in East Asia it's a whole different story. In China as well as in Japan, to have huge ears, preferably accompanied by long and thick earlobes just like Buddha, is considered a symbol of good luck, wealth, a sign of intelligence, and a long life.

As I mentioned earlier, the doctor had asked us if we wanted to take the placenta home after Fu gave birth to Luka. We politely declined. But actually it's an age-old practice in China, dating back more than 2,000 years, to eat your placenta after delivering your baby, and the practice has re-emerged over the past decade.

And as I found out, the health-giving qualities of eating the placenta is even gaining in popularity in many Western countries, where some believe it, like papaya and pig's feet, can improve the flow of breast milk, and can also help ward off postnatal depression and boost your energy levels.

Eating placentas is thought to have anti-ageing effects. The first emperor of China, Qin Shihuang, who all his life searched for immortality and among other things ate mercury, which probably helped kill him, was a big fan of eating placentas. And the infamous Dowager Empress Cixi, is also said to have been a placenta connoisseur again in order for her to achieve longevity.

While apparently only about 10 percent of parents who take the placenta home after giving birth, the number is apparently rising every year. In public hospitals they might not ask you if you want it, because they can make money selling it fresh out the back door (up to more than RMB 300 a piece) or making it into medicine. But in private hospitals it seems they will most likely ask the new parents, and many choose the option of taking home both a new born baby and a doggy bag.

While trade in the organs has been banned since 2005, you can buy it legally as dry powder or pills in pharmacies, usually mixed with other traditional medicinal herbs, but a fresh one is considered much better. It is believed to be able to fortify the '*qi*' (life energy) and enrich the blood, and it's especially good for different kinds of kidney diseases. Fu actually also once went to buy a fresh placenta from a *guanxi* (a connection) at a maternity hospital. It was for her friend's father who had kidney problems.

It is also a popular subject on many a blog on the internet. Recipes are numerous and include both smoothies, soups, tacos, dumplings, lasagne, pizza, and spaghetti and meat balls among others. If you are looking for new epicurean delights to satiate your discerning palate here is one recipe for you to try:

Hunanese placenta stew
First you clean ¼ fresh, raw placenta and 100 gr lean pork meat and cut it in to small square pieces. Then you take 20 gr wolfberry fruit, 30 gr root of the bonnet bellflower (also known as Codonopsis and *dangshen* or poor man's ginseng), 3 gr liquorice, and 2 pieces of fresh ginger, wash everything and put it all in a wok, add sufficient water to cover it and bring to a boil. After that turn down to a small to medium heat and let it simmer for about two hours. Taste and serve.

RE-EDUCATION THROUGH LABOUR

I remember reading in another book for fathers-to-be where the author asked: "What the hell do you do with a dried-up umbilical cord? Mount it on a display?" And actually, surely without having even the slightest clue about it, he was very close to the truth if he had been in China. The umbilical cord stump falls off after about a week. And then you could have asked the exact question above, and thrown it in the garbage. However, our *ayi* had a different suggestion. She suggested that we should go to the Tiananmen Gate, climb the stairs and stick it into a crack in the old painted woodwork, just like the family she had been with before had done. The higher and more important the building the better. It will supposedly be good for the baby's future prospects for both career and opportunities in life. Next time you go visit the famous landmark, be extra careful to look for little dried meat stumps sticking out here and there. You might even want to consider going there with the same goal in mind. Who knows? It might help. But after some consideration, thinking of the embarrassment of being caught by a guard while trying to fit a small stump of dried umbilical cord next to where Chairman Mao announced the People's Republic of China in 1949, we, however, put it back in the little box. But we have kept it, just for a rainy day.

While I assumed that Luka's age at birth was zero, I quickly realized that for the Chinese, being born means automatically turning one. Additionally, as Luka was born in the end of October, a year was soon added to his age on his first Lunar New Year's Day. Thus after 100 days, Luka was, according to many Chinese, now, a little confusingly, considered two years old.

We invited lots of guests to celebrate Luka's first one hundred days in the way you are supposed to according to Chinese tradition. Normally it also involves shaving off either all of the child's hair or leaving a little spot on top of the head. However, we couldn't make ourselves do that. Luka had so little hair to take (I hope he will not take after his father in this respect) and anyway not at all enough to make the otherwise traditional calligraphy brush which parents make out of their child's hair.

There is even a traditional Chinese festival for cutting the hair of babies. On the day of the Longtaitou Festival, which falls on the second day of the second month according to the lunar calendar, and means "dragon raising head", it is custom to cut the hair of babies. This will supposedly give the baby a lucky start for the New Year and mean that he or she will be blessed with a successful, long and happy life.

A German friend of mine came home to find the *yuesao* just about to shave her little daughter's beautiful hair. "If you cut even one hair on her little head, I will cut all of yours off too!" she exclaimed. The *yuesao* nearly cried and told her, "I am only trying to do my job."

But the hair is really important, and not least in the way it grows. The Chinese believe that a baby with more than one hair crown will be mischievous and disobedient as he or she grows up. Louis has four so we expect to be kept pretty busy for years to come. The looks of pity we have received from older Chinese ladies on the street when they have spotted it, I tell you! Luckily Luka only has two...

Luka's 100-day celebrations fell close to Chinese New Year. Not only was it Luka's first New Year celebrations, it was also my *benmingnian*, which in Chinese zodiac terms, means that it was the year of my Chinese zodiac sign. As mentioned earlier, I am born in the year of the tiger, and I would turn thirty-six that year.

I had for a number of years noticed and laughed a little every time the Chinese department stores yet again would be filled with big red underwear around the time of Chinese New Year. I normally quite like red underwear when it is on Fu. To quote Borat, "that's a-very nice." But I had not given much thought to the possibility that one day it would be me wearing it. Because what I came to notice was that all the large-sized red underwear I had been seeing for years, but never really looked at, was actually for men. On top of the bright red color, they were also embroidered with a gold tiger.

The number one gift for anyone turning twelve, twenty-four, thirty-six etc., was, I found out, a pair of red underwear. And if you have to wear them every day all year round which is strongly recommended, better have your sweetheart buy you more than one pair. I received ten pairs. The thing is that unfortunately the Chinese traditionally consider the *benmingnian* an unlucky year. To ward off any dangers that might befall you during this year, wearing the auspicious red jockeys should help you through it. Red is anyway one of the luckiest colors in China, symbolizing good fortune, joy, loyalty, success and happiness among others.

I should have known what was coming for me, because Fu had been wearing red underwear for a whole year, just two years earlier, and I had even given her the accompanying jade armband to ward off any malicious evil forces of the universe. I just hadn't seen it coming.

Now, wearing my new blazingly red boxers (I didn't get the kind with embroidered tigers on, but I was nevertheless very pleased that this Chinese superstition didn't say anything about it having to be a thong), I was ready to take Luka out for walks in the nearby Working People's Cultural Palace–a park to the east of the Forbidden City, protected against any kind of evil imaginable.

Braised Pork Knuckles with Soy Sauce recipe

Pig's feet, trotters or pork knuckles, dear child has many names, is classically known in China for its milk supply boosting qualities. Thus it is one of the very popular ingredients in the array of postpartum (also known as confinement) dishes in the Chinese kitchen. On top of this it is also supposed to be very good for your skin–male as well as female.

This pig's feet recipe will fill your home with heavenly aromas as it slowly cooks. The finished result is meltingly tender pork with a fantastic sauce. Many recipes also add hard-boiled chicken or quail eggs to the final dish.

The traditional way of making this dish for women is to use old ginger with its tough, woody and fibrous texture. Old ginger is supposedly good for helping women expel wind (a very Chinese term) from the abdomen and get a speedy recovery.

I have to say that I actually quite like this dish. But everything with moderation including pig's feet.

How to prepare it:

In a pot, combine enough water with half of the spring onions (30 gr), 60 g of ginger, and about 400 g of pork knuckles. You will need enough water to cover the pork knuckles. Bring to a boil on high heat. Simmer for 5 minutes. Drain completely dry and discard the green onion and ginger.

In a separate pot, combine 500 ml of chicken broth, 500 ml of water, 5 star anise, 10 g of pepper corn, 3 tablespoons of soy sauce, and 1 tablespoon of dark soy sauce. Bring it to a boil. Add the blanched pork knuckles. Simmer on medium heat for an hour. Reduce to low heat, simmer for 30 minutes. Remove from heat, then cover with the lid and allow the pork knuckles to rest inside the broth.

You can serve the pork knuckles hot or at room temperature.

You can serve the pork knuckles in medium-sized chunks or remove the bones and cut into smaller pieces. Chop the rest of the spring onions and sprinkle it on top. Ready to serve.

Another delicious dish is the Deer Antler Healing Soup
Traditional Chinese Name: (Lu rong gao li can ji tang)
A pretty traditional (although the ingredients can be difficult to find) Chinese confinement soup. High quality Korean ginseng is not a cooling ingredient and is extremely beneficial in aiding the body in healing. You can really taste the fire or "hotness" in this soup as it literally does warm your body. Here is how to prepare it: Blanch one pound (500 gr) of fresh pork shank and one fresh whole chicken (prepared) in a pot of boiling water. In a separate pot of boiling water, add 5-6 slices of cleaned deer antler, 5-6 slices of washed ginseng, and 5 large red dates together and boil on high heat for 30 minutes. Here you can either turn your soup onto medium and let it continue to simmer for another 2 hours or transfer soup into a ceramic pot and double boil for 2 hours (the objective is to intensify the flavor of the soup with the Chinese herbs). Serve it hot.

13

Xiao Hello!

After Luka was born, I was walking around the neighbourhood almost daily with him in his pram, and you might think that this was as normal in China as it is in most Western countries. It wasn't! To the surprise of most foreigners, Chinese as well as American, there are prams outside with sleeping babies everywhere in Denmark. Even during the cold winter months. Once a Danish mother was even arrested in New York for leaving the pram with her sleeping daughter outside a cafe while she was sipping coffee inside. Sometimes it was like the pram had fallen down from the moon. Mr Li, who we met looking at a new apartment, almost went into shock when, after we had pushed and carried the pram around for half an hour, he realized that there was a baby down there. "I thought you were carrying your groceries around," he said. "Groceries usually don't make crying sounds, or at least they shouldn't." I mumbled in surprise. Maybe he thought we were having something exotic for dinner?

One afternoon when I was out strolling with the infamous pram in the local park, a pretty young Chinese tour guide came towards me holding her flag high in front of a big group of local tourists who were clearly not listening to anything she was saying. But when she was less than a meter in front of me, she stopped, pointed her flag at me, and in her screeching megaphone, said to her group: "This vehicle is used by many foreigners specifically to carry around their children."

Immediately all her guests turned and looked first at the pram and then at me. Then, almost univocally they exclaimed: "Really?!!"

"It is true", I told them, smilingly, while they started to photograph the unfathomable scene in front of them.

The 'Kodak Moment' (or rather WeChat Moment) of their trip to the capital: A white Caucasian male pushing an odd looking vehicle with a little baby boy inside, looking quite Asian, but then again not quite so Asian. This was clearly something they all wanted in their photo albums. Luckily Luka just carried on sleeping.

This and numerous similar incidents became an almost daily routine. Chinese people were fascinated with my children, trying to take sneaky photos and videos of them when they thought we weren't looking (and sometimes even with us looking straight at them), and often trying to touch them or pick them up without even asking. We quickly realized that this was what we could expect as soon as we walked out of the door. In the metro, on the bus, in the park, the mall, a restaurant or just walking along the street–pretty much everywhere we went. In a panda reserve in Chengdu we even managed to take all the attention away from the main attraction; people seemed to be more interested in my children than the cute pandas! Sometimes it would simply be too much for me to take, and I would snap and tell people to put the boys down, or stop taking photos of them, or just to stay out of our way. But in the end, having seen the surprised and confused expression on the faces of people trying to "steal" my children for their "WeChat moment" on numerous occasions, I learned to live with it. Because of course they meant no harm whatsoever.

This was just one of many facts of life in China that I needed to come to terms with. Here, pointing at or touching people, even total strangers, is not considered rude. The collective Chinese mentality and the way people interact with each other gives the idea that somehow everyone is family. Strangers are addressed as uncles and aunts, grandmothers and grandfathers, sisters and brothers, and other people's children are then accordingly, most often very affectionately, called "little brother" or "little sister". So for the Chinese, picking up the child of a complete stranger is not considered impolite or inappropriate at all. And in fact, this idea of everyone being an extended family goes a long way back. All the way back to the Chinese philosopher Mencius (372-289 BC), who famously said: *"lao wu lao yi ji ren zhi"* (treat all elders as if they were your own parents), and accordingly "treat all children as if they were your own children".

And as it happens there are also obvious benefits. I am forever in debt to the many waitresses who have carried Luka and Louis around for an hour while we had dinner in a local restaurant. And just as I most often find Chinese babies and toddlers incredibly cute, so of course do the Chinese, just the other way around. The only difference being that I usually don't "steal" their children for my personal WeChat moment.

Probably the most famous line of verse from Rudyard Kipling, from the poem "The Ballad of East and West", written in 1889, is "Oh, East is East, and West is West, and never the twain shall meet". But I'm sorry Mr. Kipling, you're wrong about that one.

For several decades following the Communist Revolution of 1949, marriages between foreigners and Chinese people were extremely rare. And, as I mentioned earlier, not even a single such marriage was officially registered in 1978, two years after the disastrous Cultural Revolution had ended and Chairman Mao had passed away. Who would even think of falling in love with a foreigner, let alone marry one, when just the possession of a foreign postcard could result in thirty years in a labour camp on the accusation of being a foreign spy? However, such marriages were never explicitly banned or judged unacceptable on a racial basis. Who would have needed that anyway in such a heavily politicized, xenophobic and paranoid time in Chinese history?

For historical reasons, China is overall a very homogenous country. In general, and in the countryside in particular, Chinese people have grown up with others of very similar physical features, and many have still only seen foreigners on TV or the Internet. So considering this, it is not strange at all that the general public wants to take photos of foreigners and their children. Often they will try to give you their own child to have them pose with you, most often not to the amusement of the child. (Funnily enough, Luka, growing up in a mainly Chinese environment, could hardly see a foreigner in the street for the first three years without going into hiding. It didn't matter how I tried to convince him that I am also a foreigner). Globalization has made both the sightings of foreigners and these mixed race marriages and children more common and accepted, but still it is a relative rarity in most parts of China. And you don't have to travel far to be noticed.

Even today, you only have to go to the outskirts of Beijing, before the greeting "hello" (often pronounced as a protracted "haaaaluo", not anything like the Adele version, and followed up by the not always favorably used "*laowai*", meaning "outsider" or "foreigner"). Ten to twenty years ago, this could be heard everywhere a non-Chinese went in China. Nowadays you will mostly hear it from children or if you go to less developed or rural regions, but it is still quite common. The greeting is then repeated over and over and is usually accompanied by a giggle and a charming flush of the cheeks. However, it is now rarely heard in large cities, at least from adults. Nevertheless, if you order a cup of coffee in Starbucks, they also often just write "*laowai*" on the cup.

But one morning soon after Louis was born, I was walking him in his stroller in our compound and we saw approaching us a small group of *ayis* out walking with their respective toddlers. Without even being able to see Louis, one of the chatting ladies pointed at the stroller and while giggling said: "Xiao hello!" (Meaning "Little hello", thus assuming that I was the 'Big hello'), and without even looking at me, she was already busy discussing the obvious benefits of a mixed race child with her friends while admiring (and touching) Louis. I had to keep pushing the stroller forwards otherwise they would likely have picked him up, and I'd only just managed to get him to fall asleep!

Another day out strolling in our compound, an old grandmother kept gawking at Luka, and kept repeating to what must have been her own granddaughter, "Look, he is so cute and so good looking!" and "How can he be so good looking? He must also be very clever, because all *hunxue'er* are much cleverer than normal children".

She continued in this manner, half the time looking at Fu, the rest of the time vividly gesturing at her granddaughter who was starting to look a little uneasy. Then she asked Fu about Luka's age. And when she replied "three", the grandmother started to nag the little girl with, "Look, he is half a head taller than you, even though you are nearly five years old!" The poor girl!

Fu politely tried to ignore the grandmother because we don't think it is healthy for the children to be told they are good-looking all the time, but she kept on nagging, and just to be absolutely sure and nail even more points, she asked Fu if he was really a *hunxue'er*, of mixed blood, and when she replied positively, the

XIAO HELLO!

grandmother burst out: "So is his father a foreigner?"

Well, yes, hello!? I'm standing right next to you!

As I think the story shows, the grandmother hadn't even noticed me. Luka, the "halfling" standing next to Fu, was the center of attention and he liked it (Louis on the other hand, hated it, and when people started gawking at him, he'll say *"bu keyi"*, meaning "not okay", and quickly burst out crying). Sounding like something out of *Lord of the Rings* or a game of Dungeons and Dragons, apart from hobbits, the word "halfling" is most often used to describe a person born of a human and a parent of another race. But these *hunxue'er*, or "halflings", of which many just say of themselves, "I'm half", are treated almost as royalty in China and are very popular in advertising. With the popular Harry Potter novels and movies coming out one after the other in those days, I felt almost like I was walking with the half-blood prince.

A century ago, in British India, "Eurasian" replaced the much more derogatory term "half caste" to describe a person of mixed Asian and Caucasian descent. The term quickly caught on in the rest of the world. After China opened up to the rest of the world in the late 1970s and early 1980s, the idea of the superiority of mixed offspring has slowly taken hold. But there has always been a preference for an Asian/Caucasian mix. It has even become relatively common for successful single Chinese women to travel to the West to be inseminated with Caucasian sperm to produce so-called genetically "superior" children.

This preference was strong as the American Idol–esque TV show, "Go! Oriental Angel" in 2009, clearly showed. A twenty-year-old female participant, with a Chinese mother and an Afro-American father, but who had lived all her life in Shanghai, received thousands of mostly very negative comments. Many were very condescending and even outright racist. One 'Miss Q' went as far as to write on the blog site *Tianya*: "I cannot help but say, those coming out of the mixing of yellow and black blood are all truly ugly".

A different type of example I found on a Chinese dating site: "Hello, I like make friends. *Wo xihuan hunxue'er*". The line is the profile heading of a 24-year old Chinese girl from Guangzhou, looking for friendship and love. The curious last part translates as "I like mixed bloods", and I assume it's not a site for vampires. It could mean that she is seeking a boyfriend who is a *hunxue'er*, but it could also mean that she is looking for a foreign man, so she can have a child of mixed blood.

Despite living in China for many years, I have never had the craving to drive my own car here. The traffic is simply too chaotic and dangerous, and using the seat belt is, ironically, usually considered an insult towards the driver. Luckily, Beijing is as flat as a pancake and thus good for biking and walking, if it wasn't for its sprawling size and the many days that suffer "foggy" (read: smoggy) weather. Downtown Beijing is around 23 times larger than Manhattan. Fortunately, taxis in Beijing are cheap. But just like New York City, they are not always easy to find or successfully hailed, and, as we found out, even more difficult when travelling with children. (The Uber of China, the *Didi*, unfortunately did not really start until our last year in Beijing).

Here's a typical scenario: The taxi stopped. We were happy because we had been waiting a very long time. We got hold of Luka and Louis, bags and stroller and walked towards the taxi and opened the door. And then when I was just about to talk to him, the driver took a quick look in the rear view mirror, like he was Robert De Niro in Taxi Driver, before speeding away with screeching tires and an open door. He did not want to take us as passengers, and this was neither the first nor probably the last

XIAO HELLO!

time it will happen. It happened pretty much every time we went out. Most common, though, was the way taxi drivers adopted the now infamous stare towards the distant horizon, purposely not seeing you as they drove past with an empty cab, because picking up a family with children was *mafan* (troublesome).

I have been very close to getting into an altercation with one of these local taxi drivers, a man with a head the size and colour of a Halloween pumpkin when he began to drive away after first stopping in front of us. It can be a frustrating experience. Half the time the taxi drivers are simply "not going that direction", or going to eat, to play cards, or they just don't want to take you to your destination because there is traffic in the way. This, in a city, where the so called "rush hour" is pretty much every hour of every day. Eventually, if they do stop, there is usually not enough room in the trunk for a stroller, or even a large bag, and you can forget about a pram altogether.

Okay. Enough complaining. It's a low-paid job with long hours, after all, and with new taxi apps like Uber and Didi, it's getting even harder for Beijing's army of cabbies to make a decent living.

Most often I found out that those who stopped usually had small children or grandchildren of their own, and the main reason that other drivers didn't stop or didn't "see" us was because they were afraid of getting the inside of their taxi dirty, which could lead to fines by the taxi company inspectors. And as many Chinese toddlers didn't wear diapers (I will get back to that later) I do understand their concern very well.

I should also mention some very positive sides as well. While cabbies in Beijing are famously gregarious and don't care who they offend, I do kind of like the typical Beijing taxi driver, his (most often a man) drawl of a local accent and the way he says "qu narrr?" where to? I also love how many of them still listens to high volume history talk shows on the radio, or actually more like oral storytelling, called *pingshu*, performed by the enjoyable raspy, drawn out sandpapery voice of Shan Tianfang, doing all the different parts as well as occasional commentary himself, and who could easily fill out a one hour taxi drive. I have had a great many talks about Chinese history with the often relaxed and laid back drivers, who seem to have all the time in the world, and just like the old Manchus in Beijing, would much rather take care of their pet birds, water their small potted plants or sit around and enjoy the finer things in life all day. And most priceless: Typical for the elderly men in Beijing, they would start every sentence with the inevitable: "*Wo gaosu ni...*", which meant something like, let me tell you how things work (as you clearly don't have a clue)...

Taxi lines at airports or train stations can sometimes be hundreds of meters long. With children, a pram or a stroller you will most often be guided to the front of the line and everybody else waiting will be very understanding, and no one seems to complain even if they have been waiting for 40 minutes. In airports there are special lines for travelers with children and everybody is understanding and helpful. I am sorry to say, but this seems to be becoming a rarity in the West, and I was even once almost held back at Copenhagen Airport on charges of child trafficking.

To most foreigners, Luka does indeed look very Asian, and this has caused some misunderstandings once in a while. On a trip with Luka to Denmark, we finally arrived at Danish immigration. After giving the elderly police officer on duty my Danish passport together with Luka's Chinese passport as well as his Danish passport, and explaining to him that for visa reasons it was easier for him to use his Chinese passport when travelling out of China, he continued to look me up and down

XIAO HELLO!

suspiciously, then at Luka and then back at me several times over. I wondered if anything was wrong. Finally the policeman gave us back our passports while surprisingly exclaiming: "You never know if this could be a case of child trafficking, so we have to be very thorough."

Taking the train from Beijing to Chengdu to visit my in-laws in those days usually took around 26 hours. It now takes about 14 hours on the high-speed train. Either way, it can be a hard job to entertain two small, active children over such a long ride, but luckily they have often found playmates on the train. I actually really enjoy travelling by train in China. The old slow ones, that is. Not only do you have time to appreciate the changing landscape and get into a slower rhythm, but you also have the chance to meet friendly people from all walks of life, and I have heard many an amazing life story on a long train ride.

Then there is the little *hunxue'er* problem–they are such an exotic rarity for many people who ride trains across China that they will be stuffed full of food and sweets for hours on end. It can seem almost like a hobby, like keeping a rare bird in a cage. Travelling for so many hours on a train with our two little boys could be described as a blessing and a curse. When Chinese people travel they tend to bring lots–and I mean lots–of snacks, fruits, candy, soda, chips, cookies, smelly tofu, spicy chicken feet etc, because who wants to go hungry or run out of food all of a sudden? The other passengers noticed Luka and Louis on the train and with the best of intentions feed them constantly, just like they do with their own children. They are "family" after all, right? I've seen Luka come back to his seat several times looking like Kung-Fu Panda, trying to break his own record for the most dumplings in his mouth at once. I know they mean well, and I am eternally grateful for the numerous friendly people who have played with Luka and Louis on the long train rides, but little boys cannot say no to more cookies and sweets, and it takes days for them to calm down after all the sugar and additives.

I have tried to tell people not to feed my kids because they can't say no, but I usually lose the argument. Especially with middle aged or older women, where any kind of communication presents unique challenges. On seeing that I am a foreigner and presuming I don't understand Chinese, their tactic (I am convinced) must derive from an age-old practice from Sunzi's *Art of War*–how to pacify your opponent. Or maybe they think I am completely deaf or just plain stupid. With sheer volume, they win the debate–and some things are simply best lost in translation.

14

A SMALL STEP FORWARD

ANY MAN WHO has been to a Chinese public toilet (sometimes directly translated as "the male sex toilet" and the handicap toilet as "deformed man toilet") will have seen this sign hanging above the urinals: 向前一小步文明一大步 (*xiangqian yi xiaobu wenming yi dabu*), and it is supposed to mean something like "one small step forward for a man, one giant leap for civilization". It has many translations–two of the more curious ones I have seen were in a roadside toilet in Hebei Province, where it said: "Access Convenience Approach Civilization" and in the Shanghai Yuyuan Bazaar, where it was translated as "Close the convenient, Close to civilization", but in reality it just means "For God's sake, please move closer and try to actually hit the urinal!" Sometimes there was even an added benefit, "You can enjoy fresh air after finishing civilized urinating". Then again, since a few years before the Beijing Olympics in 2008, it has all been about "*wenming*" (civilization or being civilized), even though it's just a simple question of hitting the spot. But before it even gets that far and complicated, this is to begin with the classic clash of civilizations question for Chinese-foreign couples who have just become parents: diaper or open-crotch pants?

"I can't stand to see a two-year-old foreign child still wearing a diaper..." We were at a friend's house, and a Chinese woman from Shanghai was visiting. Fu and I looked at each other and then at Luka who was playing on the floor and obviously wearing a diaper. He was two years and 3 months. According to the Shanghai woman, we had failed miserably as parents.

So what should we do?

Before I became a father I was among those who found it a little disgusting that little toddlers were happily peeing and pooping pretty much everywhere in China. It could just be in the middle of the sidewalk and you would have to jump, or if you were luckier it would be on some poor road-side tree or plant. I would probably even wrinkle my nose while I was passing and maybe even shake my head. After Luka was born it was almost a different story altogether. One day I shocked a whole Dutch family of four quietly enjoying their lunch in a restaurant in Ritan Park in downtown Beijing, by taking Luka a few steps away from the restaurant outdoor terrace, and letting him pee on an innocent tree nearby. Smiling at them on the way back, I was trying to give them my most innocent look saying, "When in Rome…"

Once, in an absolute emergency, I have to admit that I have even helped Luka do a number two next to a roadside tree in our local neighbourhood. Shame on me, or? I should mention that *it* was removed!

Many Chinese will teach their children to pee and poop out in the open wherever and whenever they want, starting already when the child is six months old and some even earlier. "Whistle blowing" seems to be very popular in the West. But if you thought we were the first to use it, you were wrong again. The Chinese were already whistling along a long time ago. Because with the use of cue sounds, like whistles or hissing, Chinese infants are taught to empty their bladders and bowels over bowls and buckets (or pavement, grass and roadside trees) until they're old enough to squat over toilets. And miraculously soon after the little toddler will leave the diapers behind and only be using the *kaidangku*-literally the open-crotch pants (or in the case of girls wearing a dress, often nothing at all)-and never look back. For children to pee and even poop everywhere is okay, it's even considered cute, I think, and most often their parents will look at you smilingly (just as I did) and there won't be even a trace of shame on their faces. Although it could also be one of the infamous "Asian smiles", which are often used to hide embarrassment.

I still do have limits though. Hang out at a local playground for a little while and chances are you'll see more than one little guy climbing on the monkey bars with his "precious" hanging out. At first, your impulsive reaction might be, "Oh, that's cute", but one day a Chinese grandmother let her grandson pee right on the playground with its soft-padded cushions where Luka and many other children were running around, many of them not wearing shoes. When some of the parents started complaining, the granny just pretended she didn't hear it, while staring off into the infinite horizon. Not long after, the Chinese *Weibo* and news were filled with pictures of a boy who looked at least ten years old pooping on a crowded Guangzhou subway train.

But let's get back to the Romans, the open-crotch pants and the clash of civilizations again.

Even though people (or maybe it's mostly the companies making and selling diapers here) have been saying for quite some years now that China's famous split pants may soon be eclipsed by the disposable diaper, not many in my Beijing compound seem to have been listening. The *kaidangku* were still everywhere to be seen and the principle was clear: no-fuss waste disposal. They're split down the middle-in front and back, and basically they provide maximum convenience with minimum coverage.

And the Shanghai woman was not alone. Many Chinese stared with eyes filled with pity at Luka's diaper-filled behind and half-whispered in horror that "this is the foreign custom…"

That being said, it is however very obvious that more and more urban consumers are deploying the diaper and making China one of the world's fastest growing markets for the product. Just about all of the babies who grace China's new sleek parenting magazines wear diapers and annual sales have been climbing fast. Upscale stores now rarely carry split-pants outfits, instead, shelf after shelf of diapers. But I have to say, that, in a sense, it would be kind of boring if Chinese tradition was to lose the battle and the *kaidangku* disappeared altogether. To be fair, I have to admit that neither Luka nor Louis wore a real pair of *kaidangku*.

In the West, we think of it this way: the diaper catches the pee or poop. End of story! The convenience is thought to be for the adult although I don't entirely agree on this. Have you ever tried to change a curry-coloured, crappy loaded diaper on a screaming, twisting and kicking baby? No? Then congratulations for missing the experience. And by the way, somehow you won't feel like eating curry for quite some time afterwards. The Chinese thinking of this is … *eeeewwww* yucky! Our baby can't sit in his/her own poop or pee! So here comes the idea of the split-crotch pants which help facilitate this (the Chinese apparently invented both the water closet and toilet paper already 2,000 years ago, so my guess is it is at least as old), where the convenience is for the baby. They start potty training (squatting) almost from the beginning, and wow, do they become master squatters (a technique I still cannot master well). On top of this, an added benefit is that they also won't have to deal with diaper rash and the likes. However, I do wonder what it really feels like to be wearing open-crotch pants on a minus 30-degree freezing winter day with a strong head wind howling in from Siberia.

It can actually be over nearly even before it started. A journalist friend of mine who lived in Hong Kong and is married to a local lady was happy to find out that when he came back after a few weeks of being away on the job, he returned to find out that his daughter had been fully potty-trained by his mother-in-law while he was away. "I didn't have to deal with it at all. No more diapers!"

Actually, the split crotch pants have to some extent caught on in the West as well. Here, it is called "EC"–short for "Elimination Communication" — and there seems to be a growing interest among parents in this as an alternative to making your children sit around in wet and dirty diapers. There are other benefits as well: diapers are expensive, they are environmentally unfriendly, and communication-wise it is also a way of bonding and learning to read the "secret" codes of your child. I have even seen a growing interest in the West on internet forums discussing this ancient Chinese custom and also in purchasing the split-crotch pants online. And where do they find them? Yes, you are right, China. So before they stop production altogether, maybe the Chinese producers should try focusing on the lucrative high-end children's clothing market in the West.

Apparently split-crotch pants have also caught on in mountaineering, kayaking and dry suits for scuba diving. I'm just guessing they are not of the heavy cotton padded kind.

As you cannot help but be influenced by all the top-tuned potty-trained Chinese children among our friends and acquaintances, we ended up doing sort of a golden middle way. We didn't succeed as fast as most of the Chinese children around us (at least before they have turned two years old) and we still had relapses, but we probably achieved the goal a lot faster than many children in the West.

I learned a trick from my mother in law. She told me that if the boys developed problems with bed-wetting, dog meat is the answer to all your prayers. Stews, soups, everything goes– it does the trick. I have yet to try it out, but I have my doubts even though I know dog meat is a known warming and healing ingredient in many TCM recipes. I have also never actually seen dog meat for sale in my local Beijing market.

With or without the *kaidangku*, potty-training can be a daunting task and take years to perfect, and I strongly advise you to get rid of any carpets you might have, at least for the time being. They might not ever look the same again.

15

To be or not to be

THAT WAS the question. Chinese that is. Fu's phone rang. She was taking a shower, so I answered it. Without introducing herself, the otherwise friendly Chinese lady on the other end said, "Congratulations, you are having your second child, right?"

Thinking it was one of Fu's friends or acquaintances, I replied, "Thank you, yes, that's right,", and passed the phone to Fu as she came out of the bathroom.

Her face turned very pale. She put down the phone, looking both frightened and helpless.

"That was the doctor from the family planning office in our district. She told me to come down for a 'meeting'."

The cat was out of the bag. The authorities knew we were having a second child. We immediately started imagining all sorts of worst-case scenarios, having both seen and read many a horrifying story about forced abortions being carried out in China by local family planning offices. In retrospect, I can see now that this was never likely to happen to us, but there and then, it was panic stations.

"They are not going to take my baby! We move to a new secret address and we do it today!" Fu was crying and shaking. I tried to comfort her and told her that because I was a foreigner, the worst could not happen. But still, for the first few days, we were unsure of what to do. We imagined that someone, or likely a whole team of doctors and nurses dressed in white uniforms with matching white masks and hats, could be knocking on the door at any minute.

It all started after a visit to the state-run Peking Union Medical Hospital to have an ultrasound scan taken. This had automatically been reported to the authorities in our district. We later learned from Chinese friends, that if you want to keep a pregnancy secret, you have to provide the hospital with a false ID number, name and contact details. We hadn't.

We couldn't hide it anymore. We knew that Fu would be fired from her job as a university teacher if they found out she was pregnant with a second child, so we had to make a quick decision. After asking friends and acquaintances for advice we decided that Fu would go to meet with the doctor and that she would quit her job before anyone would notice. After all, our second child, because of the one child policy, would become a Danish citizen (We could have as many children we wanted as long as they all had a foreign passport and the Chinese citizenship was renounced), and if we really wanted Louis to have a Chinese *hukou*, we found out that we would have to pay a large fine, in our case amounting to about 100,000 to 120,000 yuan or $16,000-19,000, the equivalent amount of nine years of local school fees in Chengdu. (The amount would have been double if we had applied for a Beijing *hukou*). We decided that the problem could be solved and our concerns about a team of doctors and nurses showing up were unlikely to materialize. So we stayed in our apartment for the time being and Fu didn't answer any more calls.

Shortly before Louis was born, Fu finally went to their office, but for some reason, maybe a change of staff or just plain disorganization, they had misplaced her file and so this time she

TO BE OR NOT TO BE

filled in a new information sheet with a false name, address and phone number. That solved the problem for the time being.

In China, unless you belong to one of the country's ethnic minority groups or live in the countryside, you were (at least until recently), only allowed one child. It's the same for most mixed couples where the Chinese spouse is from the city, just like with Fu and myself. At least only one of your children will get Chinese citizenship and a local *hukou*.

For us and most mixed couples, the first child is no problem. Most mixed Chinese and foreign couples living in China in fact keep both Chinese and foreign citizenship for their first born (even though dual citizenship is not officially recognized in China) for practical reasons such as visa and school fees. But here was the small obstacle: because Louis, our second-born, was born in China with one Chinese parent, and as any other child with one Chinese parent, he is by law Chinese.

It does not matter if you have not even considered giving him or her Chinese citizenship and the child, like Louis, has a foreign passport. Due to China's family planning policy we could only have one child with Chinese citizenship (without paying a fine), and as our number two, Louis, like his older brother, was Chinese by birth right, we had to try to renounce Louis' Chinese citizenship. Thus, about three months after Louis was born, we went to Chengdu.

The sign on the third floor of the Sichuan Public Security Bureau Exit-Entry Management Department in Chengdu said "Dual Citizenship" in English. A big building in the center of the city, it is located right next to one of the few remaining larger-than-life Mao statues in China, standing tall like an old communist relic near modern shopping malls, a McDonald's restaurant and a Starbucks. This is where all foreigners in Chengdu with visa problems have to go. However, in Chinese it said *"guoji chongtu"* meaning "nationality problems or conflict". Dual citizenship is in fact neither recognized nor allowed for Chinese citizens. And as the Chinese sign suggested, it was going to be a problem.

The reason we were doing this in Chengdu and not Beijing is because citizenship has to be applied for in the city where the Chinese parent has his or her *hukou*, therefore we had to travel 2,200 kilometers, then more than 26 hours on a train, a mode of transport we chose to save money. We quickly realized that a single trip would be far from enough; a quick search on the internet and asking friends who had been in the same situation, revealed that it would be a tough job getting rid of Louis' Chinese citizenship so he could become legally regarded as a foreigner. It became clear that the Middle Kingdom was not going to let go of him easily, and not without a fight.

Realizing that the process of renouncing Louis' citizenship would take a while, we asked at the Beijing Public Security Bureau (PSB) and were assured that the rules stated that we could get up to three exit-entry permits for Louis. This is a small passport-like booklet that allows a Chinese-foreign baby born in China to pass immigration leaving China, and we could get it while applying for his renunciation of his Chinese citizenship. This would enable us to leave China for the summer and Christmas holidays during the coming year, because as long as he was considered a Chinese citizen, he would not get a visa in his Danish passport. We had a great idea to go to Hong Kong for a summer dim sum / Disney World combo. As we would now be going to Chengdu anyway to apply for a visa for both Fu and Luka (you still need a visa to go to Hong Kong as a Chinese citizen and you can only apply for the visa where you have your *hukou*) it seemed like the perfect plan.

The Chinese proverb *Shan gao, huangdi yuan*, meaning "The

TO BE OR NOT TO BE

mountains are high and the emperor is far away", is very suitable in the case of Sichuan, a province surrounded by high mountain walls on all sides. Throughout Chinese history it led quite a secluded life until the mid-20th century, because of its geographic isolation and inaccessibility. And so in Chengdu, as in any other Chinese city far away from the "emperor" and the country's capital, we found that the rules were just not the same.

So while Fu and Luka had gone up to the third floor to wait in line to ask about Louis' nationality problem, here I was standing outside in line with hundreds of Chinese who clearly had had the same wonderful idea of going to Hong Kong for the summer. It was a typical hot and humid Chengdu summer morning and Louis was sitting in his baby carrier on my chest.

Standing in line is a way of life in China. Because of the huge population, long queues to get into the subway, on the bus, in public hospitals, into museums, and to visit any kind of tourist attraction like Mao's mausoleum on the Tiananmen Square or the Forbidden City, which on peak season days see more than 180,000 visitors in one day, is just a normal everyday thing for millions of Chinese. After numerous times standing in line for the mausoleum with thousands of Chinese, to catch a glimpse of the embalmed body of The Great Helmsman in his glass coffin, Fu, one day, disappointingly told me that everybody at her university knew that their professor made the very realistic wax figure. Not long ago, during the Mao era until the late 1970s, standing in line for food or clothes using ration coupons was common. If you did not jump the queue, or at least try to get a better spot, it could mean that you would go hungry that day. During the 1980s and 1990s, food scarcity was eliminated, but instead it was replaced by a shortage of quality service and luxury consumer items, among other things. The Chinese who experienced the days when everything was in shortage except big political campaigns, still vividly remember it, and thus it is not strange that they cut the queue if they can. Today, as many of our Chinese friends and relatives often complain about and also miss, there is not much left of communist comradeship in China, and it is every man (or family) for himself. Seize that seat on the metro or there will be none, seize that spot in the kindergarten or there will be none. Seize that Ferrari or there will be none. Many of the luxury car dealers in downtown Beijing are often empty because supply simply cannot keep up with the demand. You get the picture.

However, before and during the Olympics in 2008, the Beijing authorities did an impressive job, during their "civilize the people" campaign, when suddenly everybody was told to stand in line for the bus, metro, tickets etc. and posters all over the city declared that "Civilization is the most beautiful scenery". It was rather successful, I must say, and I sometimes catch myself missing the fun of queuing with the chaotic pushing, shoving and cutting in line "old style".

The line moved incredibly slowly and I started to sweat profusely. After about two hours, a soaking wet t-shirt and an understandably very unhappy baby, I finally got the chance to hand in an application form for a Hong Kong summer break. I received the message: "You are now waiting in line as number 566."

The application included me copying two sheets of Chinese text by hand, among other things, promising that we would all return to the mainland after our little getaway. I went back to the hotel with the boys and waited for another four hours after lunch, and finally, just about five minutes before closing time, our application went through.

Almost at the same time, however, Fu came back with the disheartening news that we were only given *one* exit and re-entry permit for Louis. Only one! Realizing that if we were to go to

TO BE OR NOT TO BE

Hong Kong we would not get an extra chance of taking Louis out of China for our planned Christmas holiday trip to Denmark, we had spent a whole day in vain. Permits to go to Hong Kong arrived a week later. Great!

That evening Fu tried to explain what little the staff had said about Louis' nationality problem and we spent the evening discussing the procedure. But we had to conclude that we still had more questions than answers. So the next morning we were back in line behind the Mao statue.

On the way in, we passed a sign on the stairs saying: "Your Entry and Exit Needs a Permit–But Our Service Is of No Limit". But the reaction from the lady behind the massive desk, when we approached a second time to ask about the rules for renouncing Louis' Chinese nationality, was: "They are back, again!?"

We were slightly set back by the comment, as nothing had been clear the day before, and my blood pressure was on the rise. But slowly we realized, after waiting for quite some time seeing staff members going up and down the hall way and in and out of several offices, that the staff did not have a clue what to do, as they had actually never dealt with our specific situation before.

Finally we were shown into a smoke-filled office. This was the domain of Captain Li, a friendly man in his mid-fifties with alert black eyes, and an open, almost innocent face and wavy black hair. While he chain-smoked his Sichuan Pride cigarettes, he patiently listened to our story and was very understanding and sympathetic. He promised to help as much as he could and make sure Louis' case was pushed forward in the system. He assigned the pretty, young female officer Miss Yang to our case. Now we had one "*guanxi*" (a personal connection or contact), or maybe even two, inside the bureaucracy.

Both Li and Yang did their best, but of course they could not make miracles happen overnight. We asked if they did not have a handbook on how to do this, but the discouraging answer was that unfortunately such a thing did not exist. Instead they told us: "You had better go back and prepare everything."

"Excuse us, but what is everything?" we replied.

"Just prepare everything," was the disheartening final answer.

It was time for lunch, and the office would be closed again.

We came back after lunch with pretty much everything we could think of and presented the package to Miss Yang, and nervously awaited her verdict.

She told us that there were two problems. Both were our own fault. One was that we had to have Fu's *hukou* updated, as it stated that she was still single. After finally finding the right office at the other end of this city of more than ten million people, we actually walked out again having successfully achieved this after only fifteen minutes, almost in disbelief, but in a very good mood. They had updated Fu's *hukou* there and then. Maybe there was hope for Louis case yet.

The second problem was that I had forgotten to register with the local Public Security Bureau where my in-laws live. So we went back to the suburb where my in-laws live.

We finally found the local police station, but we probably arrived at a bad time, because most of the station staff was sleeping or simply just not there. We awoke one police officer and asked him about the foreigners' registration. He showed a board outside with the names and mobile phone numbers of his colleagues and told us to call Mr. Wang. I asked if it was really up to us to call the officer in charge, surely it would be an internal call within the department? I was wrong. We called the number, but it went unanswered. We looked around the building, but most offices were either empty or the officers were sleeping on top of their computers and desks. (I have always admired how most Chinese seem to be able to instantly fall asleep anywhere).

TO BE OR NOT TO BE

After waking up a few uncooperative police men and women, we ended up with the same conclusion: Only Mr. Wang could do this. Nobody else had any idea what to do, and had no access to the right documents.

We continuously called Wang's mobile, and finally he answered with a slightly annoyed *"Wei, shi shei?"* (Hello, who is it?). We could hear the clattering of mah-jong pieces in the background. Unfortunately, he explained, he was very busy the rest of the afternoon and could not make it back to the station before it was time to call it a day anyway. We told him the whole story and finally he agreed to leave his game and come back to the station. We waited patiently.

When he finally got back and switched on the computer, there was another problem. The form stated that I was adopted (I am not), and there was no way to delete that from the template. We all laughed.

It also stated that even though I am not particularly green, I was an "alien", and as such had to register temporary accommodation.

But, green, adopted or not, the application was finally accepted.

A few months later, we were back again in the Sichuan Public Security Bureau Exit-Entry Management Department, asking if there had been any progress with Louis' case of having his Chinese nationality revoked. The unpromising answer from Miss Li was "not yet".

This time, however, probably because we now had a *guanxi* there, both Miss Li and all the other staff members we encountered were all much more helpful and understanding. She explained to us that such an application would go from the city to the provincial level until it finally reached the state level in Beijing where it would be handled and processed until it was ready to go back through every level all the way back to the office in Chengdu again. We needed to be patient, she explained, as it would probably take a year at least. But fortunately she had an idea.

She asked us if we had any plans to leave China and go to Denmark for the Christmas holiday. When we replied "yes", she explained to us that the way forward with Louis' case of "nationality problem" and beat the system, so to speak, was to apply for an exit and entry permit and then take him to Denmark. Here, we should go to the Chinese embassy and apply for a Chinese tourist visa for him with his Danish passport. Supposing that went smoothly, because, according to her, there were (at the time) no corresponding systems between Chinese embassies abroad and the authorities within China, we could just go to the authorities in Beijing after coming back to China again, and register him under my work and residence permit. It sounded like a great plan. But of course, life (and sneaky ideas to beat the system) doesn't always go according to plan.

We took an early flight to Denmark for the holidays, leaving ample time to apply for the visa. Everything went smoothly, just as she had predicted, and Louis received his L Visa (valid for 30 days) only four days later, just in time for Christmas, which we now could enjoy with peace of mind. Perfect.

Or so we thought. We came back to Beijing in early January and were full of optimism when we went once again to the Public Security Bureau, a massive grey building located, conincidentally or not, close to where the former Andingmen city gate, a name which means "securing peace", once stood. But one quick look from the officer behind the desk quickly sealed the fate of Louis' case and shot down any hopes we had had about a smart solution to the problem. It did not matter what an officer

TO BE OR NOT TO BE

had recommended in far-away Chengdu. This was Beijing, and without an official renunciation of his Chinese citizenship, I might as well throw his Danish passport and tourist visa in the garbage because Louis was still Chinese. We had in fact broken the law by getting a Chinese visa in his Danish passport, and since he was Chinese, the visa was useless anyway. And it would now be impossible to leave the country again, because we had used up the only chance for Louis to leave China, before his application went through.

16

Fifty Shades

The conversation started something like this: "I would like to look at an expensive perfume." And then I couldn't help myself. "Let's cut to the chase. We would like to buy a perfume to suit a fifty-something-year-old kindergarten headmaster, and it should be expensive enough to get our son into that kindergarten."

The shop owner looked at me a little strangely, but she knew exactly what I was talking about, and giggled nervously. It seemed I was definitely not the first customer to ask her something like this, even if I was probably more blunt than most.

I know that giving gifts to your child's kindergarten or school teacher is quite common also in Europe and in the United States, but there it is usually done, I believe, in order to show appreciation for a job well done, or to say thank you for the way a difficult time for the child and the family was handled. And, it is most often given, when the child is leaving the institution. And last of all, gifts are small and given openly. It is more the thought that counts, and the wording of the accompanying card or note.

But in our case, Luka had not even started kindergarten properly before the gift-giving began. The way Beijing municipality officially locates spaces for children in the city's public kindergartens are first and foremost by *hukou*. Those with a Beijing *hukou* living in the local district have first priority.

Then come people who have bought an apartment or house in the area, and only third come people like us with no local *hukou* and no property in the area. Officially that is. But of course there are ways to circumnavigate these guidelines, as long as you are dedicated enough in your "voluntary" support of the local educational unit. However, we had a hard time finding out exactly how dedicated we needed to be, so we asked around and searched the internet to learn about the experiences of other parents. We discovered that 30,000 RMB (about $4,000) would not be enough to get Luka into the local kindergarten close to my office building, a place that had been recommended to us. A blog post by a father of a prospective student revealed angrily that even after he had "voluntarily" donated 30,000 RMB, he was deemed to be not sincere enough in his support. Needless to say, the student was not admitted, nor was the money returned.

Other friends told us about their experiences and advised us to try with an amount equivalent to a year's kindergarten fees, typically about 15,000 yuan (around $2,000). But what if this amount would be considered too low? And even if we gave more, who to give it to? The headmaster, the bookkeeper, one of the senior teachers? We did not know, nor did we know how to find out. It's not like one can say, "Excuse me, who is the unofficial official bribe-taker in this institution?" It was a very grey area indeed.

Xiao Gao, a friend of mine, once placed five envelopes with gift certificates worth 5,000 RMB each in the individual pockets of her son's kindergarten teachers. Her son was just starting in public kindergarten, but she wanted to make sure that he was looked after properly and dressed appropriately, whatever the season and condition, all in the hope that he would receive a little extra attention from the teachers. But what if the parents of the boy next to him gave an even greater contribution? When does it all end? Apparently not any time soon.

In China, education has long been considered the key to getting ahead in an exceedingly competitive society. And, as Xiao Gao's story shows, parents will use all means available to give their offspring a head start. Greasing the wheels, gift-giving, bribery, corruption, call it what you want, it starts early, and it has been around through many dynasties. "Corruption is the oil that makes this deeply defective machine possible; corruption is not just a little bit of grit in the machine," said University of Hong Kong professor, Frank Dikötter about China. "It is the backbone of the economy of the country."

I had personally experienced it several times before. Once, I discovered I had visa problems because the authorities doubted the authenticity of examination diplomas from my Danish university. This was smoothed over with 6,000 RMB (around US$1,000) given to visa officials I never actually met face to face. President Xi Jinping's campaign against corruption has strong public support, but it is has also hampered the economy with many local officials hesitant about making decisions and signing off on new projects. Incentives are not so readily available as before. Who is clean and who will tell?

Not surprisingly, Chinese proverbs about corruption are plentiful. *"Da ji bu chi sui mi"*, translates as "Big rooster eats no small rice". Another one goes: "A man can never be perfect in a hundred years; but he may become corrupt in less than a day." Officially, most public servants in China earn very little. A monthly salary of US$350 to US$550 is standard, and even high-ranking officials (the big roosters) see only a relatively small pay check by Western standards. However, they often have tremendous power over other people's lives, and large sums of money pass through their hands every day, which is a potentially dangerous combination.

Teachers in public kindergartens and schools in China receive only limited pay for their hard work. And education is no exception to the rest of the Chinese society where corruption is pervasive. It is perhaps not so surprising that some of the administrators and teachers would like a piece of the pie.

We learned from friends that gifts were expected not only to get into the kindergarten, but also to be given on official Teachers Day (September 10th), and holidays like National Day and New Year, and then simply on a regular basis to keep the wheels running, and not to lag behind the amount of gifts from other parents. How much would it amount to in a year? We had no idea.

A friend of ours, Miss Wang, had a ten-year-old son in the fourth grade. She told us how the teachers at his son's school in Chengdu had started an after-hours class program in which they had to pay for him to attend. She says that during the school day, teachers intentionally leave out key parts of the curriculum, and only by paying extra did she know for sure that her son had been taught everything he needs to know for the exams.

An anonymous employee at China's prestigious Tsinghua University revealed to the *New York Times* that a donation of 150,000 yuan ($25,000) could secure a spot in the Clean China Kindergarten affiliated with the famous university. Officially, the kindergarten is only for children of staff. Both international and Chinese media were for a time full of stories about how more or less 'voluntary donations' to secure a spot in the right institution, or get a head start, a front row seat, preferential treatment or better grades, has reached extreme levels in the past decade in China.

But as one Chinese kindergarten teacher wrote on a popular Chinese Q&A website, Why do parents present gifts and red envelopes of money? What do they expect? And how does it make the individual teachers feel? She said she thought many parents gave gifts just to be on the safe side, not to be seen in a bad light, or because they believe their child would receive preferential treatment. Moreover, they give out of fear, that if they didn't, their child might be given less attention, be maltreated or even tyrannized in the kindergarten. She then went on to make a very thought-provoking calculation: In an average classroom with two teachers and a child-care worker, there are 25 children. Normal hours are from 8 am to 4 pm, and, not accounting for the two hour post-lunch break when the children take their nap, it means every teacher can only offer at most 14 minutes and 40 seconds personal time with each child during the day, if shared equally. She concludes that it is simply not possible to give every child "special" treatment. Many parents believe they have to bribe, but frequently it becomes awkward and puts the teacher in a difficult position. Often the bribes are unasked for and unwelcome. As another kindergarten teacher puts it, "It is a headache. If you refuse, then parents might wonder why, and if you take it they might also start talking." She concluded that "the best gift parents can give us is their confidence, respect and cooperation."

Before Luka was old enough for kindergarten, he attended a pre-kindergarten class in the local establishment just behind our compound for a few hours a week. He, I think, got in because he is a *hunxue'er* (of mixed blood). Kindergartens like to look good for prospective parents, so if a child has special talents like Kung-Fu, calligraphy, dancing, or in our case, mixed blood, the chances of getting your son or daughter into the local kindergarten should be a lot better.

But just because he was accepted in to pre-kindergarten, it

did not mean that we could count on a spot for him when it came to real kindergarten starting at three years old. Hence the trip to the perfume shop.

We visited almost every kindergarten in a radius of about two or three kilometers from our home, knocking on gates installed between security fences (kindergartens are all very well guarded due to a series of attacks on kids over the years, usually by a troubled individual with a knife), but prospects were bleak.

We decided to look at private options, and I went to see the International Ivy School Kindergarten on the first floor of my office building. Each time I passed the door it reminded me of the movie Forrest Gump, because of a sign on the door saying "Multiple intelligences". It was much too expensive, but in the end we found a great private Chinese kindergarten called *Huijia* (meaning something like "gather beautiful things"), where fees were reasonable (although we still had to dig into our savings) and expectations were clear to begin with. I am happy to say that we were all very happy with it, Luka included. And I think that the annual fee was surely much less than what all the 'voluntary' gifts in the public kindergarten would have amounted to.

Luckily it seemed that everyone was getting sick of the situation, and things started to change for the better. When looking at Chinese online forums discussing this issue, many parents now choose not to give gifts or bribe anymore. In fact, in some schools, teachers were turning the tables by giving out small cash prizes to students taking the final high school exams (*gaokao*). This might well be a publicity stunt, of course, and there's still a long way to go. But with the anti-corruption campaign of recent years, hopefully parents in the future won't be faced so frequently with this confusing and undesirable situation when it is time for their children to start kindergarten.

17

WHO'S WHO?

WHEN FU and I married, I got a new set of parents, so to speak. I was all of a sudden expected to start calling them (not surprisingly) "*mama*" (mother) and "*baba*" (father) respectively, which seemed a little odd and, I must admit, was rather difficult to get used to in the beginning. That being said, you might be excused for thinking that names for family member in China are very simple. They are not! Actually quite the opposite is the case, and I, for one, am still often confused.

Traditionally, families in China have followed patriarchal lines, and the extended family tree is generally much more significant in China than in most Western countries. This also adds more importance to how people are related, which leads to different names both for whether or not they are older than the speaker and also, very importantly, whether one is related by paternal or maternal relatives. The words denoting the relative relationship for family members on the father's side are completely different from the names on the mother's side, and in some cases several names can be in use at the same time. For instance, the word for grandfather on the mother's side can be both '*waizufu*', '*waigong*', and '*laoye*'. The character 外 '*wai*' means outside or even foreign, but it's also used to indicate that someone is outside the paternal bloodline. As such, both Luka and Louis are '*waisun*', meaning "grandsons outside the family' to Fu's parents, and so both Fu and our boys should worship my ancestors. However, since we don't practice ancestor worship in Denmark, we believe it is okay for the children to honour the Deng family's ancestors. In China, it is seen as the highest expression of filial piety.

During Qingming Festival, known in English as Tomb Sweeping Day, in early April, we always went to make offerings to the family ancestors, and literally clean and sweep their tombs. As mentioned earlier, Fu has an older brother who has a son, just one year younger than Luka, so the continuation of the male bloodline in the Deng family should be safe. As Qingming Festival also witnesses one of the busiest traveling periods in China, even rivaling the notoriously chaotic period over Chinese New Year, we often try to go a few days before or after. Even though the direct male bloodline is most important, our children also take part in the festival. Kneeling in front of the ancestors gravestones, they kowtow and make offerings to the dead, lighting incense sticks and candles, as well as bring flowers, cigarettes, fruits and other foods.

Looking around us, we saw other families placing whole meals of Sichuan sausage, smoked bacon, and other dishes, as well as bowls of noodles and rice including chopsticks. Next to it, they placed cups or small bottles of alcohol. Ancestors are considered the intermediaries between humans and the gods, and honoring them is a method to appease the spirits and avoid their angry return among the living in the form of ghosts. We also burn stacks of paper money, called 'Hell money', often with denominations of millions and billions on them. They are printed to resemble real bank notes, but their sole intended purpose is to be offered to the deceased ancestors as a solution to resolve their possible financial problems in the so-called 'underworld prison'. We have also lighted firecrackers every year to scare away evil spirits, but after air pollution has become a serious problem in China, in many graveyards it is no longer allowed to burn or light anything. Not even food is allowed anymore because of the mice and rats, with flowers the only offering allowed. I am sure it is good for the air quality, but definitely bad news for the dead ancestors, and also makes it much less interesting. I like it that in China it is the unwritten rule that every living Chinese is only responsible for three generations of dead forefathers' and their well-being in the afterlife, so pragmatic as the Chinese are, it doesn't get out of hand.

In China, 'family' is a rather comprehensive concept. Even strangers who are unrelated are addressed as younger / older brothers or sisters, aunts, uncles and grandmother… even father! Therefore, when you marry a Chinese spouse you not only got a new set of "parents", but maybe also new 'brothers' and 'sisters' (although less likely if he or she was born in the 1980s after the one child policy started). And don't forget all the complete strangers you will have to address as *"shushu"* (uncle), *"ayi"* (aunt), *"gege"* (big brother) or *"meimei"* (little sister) etc. Because, remember? We are all one happy family in China.

The use of family titles for strangers is, however, superficial. Real family always comes first. Chinese tend to view society in terms of insiders and outsiders, and most view their world in terms of their web of connections, called *guanxi*, and the hierarchical order is: family, personal and professional network, and then everyone else. In other words, the Chinese–consciously or not–see the world in terms of two groups of people: Their own circle of relationships on one side and everyone else on the other. Many of our Chinese friends have pooled together large sums of money within their families just to send the brightest young man or woman in the family away for studying abroad, to buy an apartment, a tractor, or a piece of land etc. all because of the strong commitment to their families.

Compared to most western cultures, Chinese society, with its age-old strong belief in Confucianism, has always had a strong focus on family and a much stronger distinction between "in" versus "out" groups. In practise that means that, in general, the Chinese can seem to be cold, indifferent, suspicious or sometimes even hostile towards strangers (many unhelpful civil servants whether in Denmark, in China or anywhere else, also seem to fall in this category). Stated simply: Taking care of your own takes front seat. It is understandable in the Chinese context where life and survival has often been uncertain during war, civil war, mass campaigns, hunger, and millions of dead people. Where neighbors accused neighbors, children spied on parents and students incriminated their teachers all in the name of revolution or just the right political spirit, and it could result in thirty years in a prison camp or even death. But still it surprised me numerous times that what I believed was common courtesy such as holding doors, getting up if a pregnant woman enters the bus, helping an elderly citizen carry their groceries, or helping someone who accidentally fell on his or her bike etc., more often than not, I found that I or other foreigners were the only ones that actually did any of this. To this "odd" behaviour, some of my Chinese friends have noted that they think that many westerners seem to treat complete strangers like friends, but on the other hand sometimes treat family like strangers.

It has, however, always stupefied me how my Chinese family and friends most often avoid telling relatives and especially parents and elders about even terminal illnesses or other huge personal challenges in life. I know that it is often done for the sake of not overly worrying parents or for preserving face or peace, but still find it must be equally hard to live with the knowledge that you yourself or your father or grandmother is terminally ill, but you cannot tell anyone in your family.

In China, it has also had the consequence that philanthropy was a largely unknown phenomenon or at least in reality for most people, although the propaganda machine always have found the most incredible stories of human sacrifice, and the unstoppable Chinese communist hero, who always serves the people (*wei renmin fuwu*), comrade Lei Feng, continuously and miraculously pops up in every other new self-sacrifice-campaign. But the internet, its online shopping where you can easily donate a small amount to the, now hundreds of new charities, have effectively changed that. After public confidence was undermined following a series of scandals involving the Red Cross Society of China and China Charity Federation, among others, (particularly after the 2008 Sichuan earthquake), the good news is that philanthropy in China is also on the rise and goes up every year.

The flip side of the coin of all this families sticking together is that even though I know it is supposed to show concern and caring, sometimes Chinese families, that being parents, grandparents, cousins, uncles and aunts, pretty much any relative (real or imagined) seem to make it his or her proudest obligation to comment (read: meddle in) on everything from clothes, appearance, grades, marital status or the lack of it, pregnancy, or your children's behaviour. It can be a little overwhelming, for anyone, I believe.

And even though it seems quite easy to start calling your parents-in-law mother and father, and your brother-and sister-in-law brother and sister, it does take some time to get used to. After spending so many years in China, I still get confused when the talk turns to family relations and all those innumerable titles for family member relationships. And while this naturally can appear complicated to most Westerners, it is still is incredibly important to the Chinese family structure. Understandably,

WHO'S WHO?

however, many Chinese also have difficulty remembering them.

The sad light on the horizon is that, with the average family size having shrunk significantly in the last thirty years, quite a number of the names are much more rarely used these days.

18

NO TIME FOR LOSERS

MUCH HAS BEEN said and written about the 'Tiger Mom' phenomenon, after Amy Chua, the American-Chinese mother of two daughters and professor of law at Yale, published her widely discussed book *Battle Hymn of the Tiger Mother*. It created an uproar in the United States and raised a storm among parents throughout the Western world even before it was published. The online version was read more than a million times even before publication.

"Chinese parents can do things that would seem unimaginable — even legally actionable — to Westerners. Chinese mothers can say to their daughters, 'Hey fatty — lose some weight'," Amy Chua explained in an article in the *Wall Street Journal*.

Maybe that is why, whenever I return to Beijing from a holiday, Chinese colleagues and friends will always start out by saying, "You've gained weight." I am sure they are right, but it is not always the thing you want to hear. At first, I must admit that I was a little annoyed by their honesty, until I learned that it was considered a term of endearment. I even started to use it myself as an after-holiday greeting. Anyway, Chua continued: "Western parents have to tiptoe around the issue, talking in terms of 'health' and never ever mentioning the f-word, and their kids still end up in therapy for eating disorders and negative self-image."

NO TIME FOR LOSERS

Chua summed it up: "Western parents are concerned about their children's psyches. Chinese parents aren't."

It came out in January 2011, shortly after Luka turned one. I was of course particularly curious, so I read her book and was astonished at what I could be up against. For instance, here are some of the things Chua's two girls were not to permitted to do: attend a sleepover, have a play date, be in a school play, watch TV or play computer games, get any grade less than an A; not be the number one student in every subject, play any instrument other than the piano or violin, not play the piano or violin.

I could further glean from all this that holidays must be spent mastering the coming semester's curriculum by heart, and that the only activities my children should be permitted to do are those in which they can eventually win a medal; and that medal must be gold. Another way to show this is the way that grading in Chinese schools work in real life: A = Average; B = Below average; C = Can't have dinner; D = Don't come home; and finally, an F = Find a new family. In short: "No time for losers!"

We also quickly started feeling the heat. When Luka was only nine months old, we started getting calls from Chinese friends asking us if we wanted to sign him up for a local baby crawling competition. Prizes were up for grabs, they said. We declined, and got a call later telling us that their daughter had won first prize (I don't know exactly what she won).

A few months later; the same mother called and asked how many Tang dynasty poems Luka could recite. Their daughter had already mastered quite a number by heart. Before age two and a half, many of the local Chinese children could already recognize and read hundreds of Chinese characters, do simple math, and had already started to play the piano and violin (at least it seemed that way to us). We soon realized that our other friend had probably given up on us, since she stopped calling.

But feeling the pressure, we started to search for extracurricular activities for Luka. We took him to music class once, but we failed miserably as parents and him as a kid, as he could not sit still when the music started playing. All the other children just sat still on their little stools while Luka started to jump up and down and literally shake his booty.

We went to a Saturday gymnastics class with Luka which was actually great, but it was also incredibly expensive and I must say a little scary. As we were getting ready to leave, I eavesdropped on the Chinese father next to me telling his daughter to hurry up because they were going to swimming class next. And don't forget, he added, "you have English class this afternoon." I was exhausted just listening to their programme for the day.

I soon realized that this girl was not alone. After Luka started kindergarten we often wanted to set play dates with the Chinese children in his class. However, this was often near to impossible because the other children were all busy doing extracurricular activities, practising violin or piano, or else they simply weren't allowed to go out and kick a ball around or just 'play'.

When, on a rare occasion, Luka had a Chinese friend over, they often looked dumbfounded at Luka's Lego bricks, and one time, the mother matter-of-factly exclaimed: "I am sorry, he doesn't know how to play with Lego". Only afterwards, I noticed that many Chinese started sending their kids to-the new talk of the town-expensive "learn how to play with Lego"-classes. Amazing!

Coming from Denmark, where most parents, rightly or not, go by the "children-play-until-they-are-old-enough-to-go-school" philosophy. (And preferably go to a 'forest kindergarten' to get your hands-on nature experience and maybe kill the chicken before you cook it). I'm still unsure of what is best for my boys. As many of our friends have realized, the Tiger Mom approach is, at least to some degree, everyday life for the vast majority of Chinese and foreign children who attend a Chinese kindergarten or school here. Thus, many parents who choose, for cost reasons or otherwise, to send their children to local kindergartens, have to embrace, or at least accept, the Chinese way. Because how else will your child hold their own in the competitive world of China?

In China, children with a knack for sports are often extracted and sent to special schools to be trained and learn how to win gold medals. During middle school, Fu was drafted for the Sichuan Province Kayaking Team just because of her build and height. Not because she liked kayaking or was good at swimming. In fact, she couldn't even swim at the time. She did not come through though, so we will never know if she could have won an Olympic gold medal for China. But luckily, not all little Chinese boys and girls are expected to win medals. There are also other ways to strike gold.

Fu was out walking in our neighbourhood when she overheard a father from our local community with his four-year-old daughter. They were in the public playground and the girl was trying to grab the metal bar to do some sort of gymnastics. She called out to her father to help her. He simply replied: "You don't have to do gymnastics, this is only for workers. You are not going to be a worker!"

The same guy told me: "I know what Chinese men want — a pretty wife who knows how to dress well, with a little culture and education, but not as much education as a PhD." He added: "My daughter will marry a man of nobility." I pointed out that there is no such thing as nobility in China, in the European sense anyway. The man explained. "She will marry the son of a party official or a rich private entrepreneur." He called the latter a *"fu'erdai"* which means someone who is second generation rich, and refers to the children of the nouveau riche. Her future seems to have been settled.

When Luka was going through the "terrible twos", we got many looks on the street when he went into a rage flip or when he was crying uncontrollably. According to many Chinese we have met, this does not happen to Chinese children. Is it a phase that Chinese children, with the help of their parents, can skip altogether? I wonder. In my case, of course, it could be due to the poor little guy having half his genes from an uncultured father belonging to a long line of barbaric Vikings.

As mentioned earlier, one of the ways that Chinese parenting is very much different from most Western countries, is the way many Chinese parents believe that praising or spoiling a child is not good and could even attract misfortune. Often when I comment on the good looks or merits of Chinese children, their parents will continuously deny it. "No, no, he's ugly, slow, stupid, fat, misbehaved...", would be some of the common answers whenever I try to praise their children. The farthest many of them go in the way of praising their children will be a "*guai*", meaning obedient, or a "*laoshi*" which can be translated as sincere and honest. Is this the answer to my question above?

It continues when they grow up. The usual response you'll get when you praise an elaborate and delicious homemade meal at a Chinese friends' house which clearly took days to prepare, is that the host will apologetically exclaim that this is just plain and boring food, and every one of your compliments will be deferred with persistence.

But honestly, living in China, it often feels like Chinese parents are able to raise stereotypically successful children: little Einsteins, math whizzes and musical geniuses. But of course, that is not the whole truth.

NO TIME FOR LOSERS

Our friends, Mikkel and Afu, a Danish/Chinese couple living in Beijing, put their eldest son into a Chinese school with an international department. From the start he excelled and was soon number one in his class, but after a while his attention started to wander into other areas of interest besides school work. Suddenly he was only number seven in his class, and immediately the school called an emergency meeting with his parents. What had gone wrong? Would this downward spiral continue or would they pull themselves and their son together and fix this temporary problem?

Similarly, Chinese friends of ours had decided that their son, very unconventionally, would be allowed to play all the way up to the first year of the local public school system. Big mistake. When he started school, the parents were immediately called in for an emergency meeting with the teachers and headmaster. All the other children could already read and write, so he was therefore last in his class, and getting scolded by teachers and teased by the children every day. He was sent to special classes to catch up. Being last in your class is not fun for anyone.

I, for one, could only just about write my name when I started in school at age six, and, as I remember it, homework didn't really start until sixth or seventh grade, and except for a few subjects that I really liked and excelled in, I was probably a very average student in most classes. My parents and I would definitely have failed according to the Tiger Mom model.

My four-year old nephew in Chengdu answered the phone by proclaiming: "My name is Xi Jinping". We all laughed, but he also knows the names of every member of the Chinese Communist Party's top organ, the Politburo Standing Committee. On the one hand, I don't know how he does it, particularly as, to a Western eye, the leaders look almost indistinguishable: same expressionless gaze, same glossy black pudding bowl hair, and the same tailor. On the other hand, I can't help finding it a little scary that he, at such a young age, is already starting to be molded into the image promoted by the Chinese propaganda machine. I must admit that we don't know if it is something he has learned just by watching TV or if he has learned it at the kindergarten.

It is simply something that we would be willing to accept if our children would both attend a local kindergarten or school. Milo, who is the son of a good friend of mine, came home from his Chinese kindergarten, where he is the only foreigner, singing loud and clear, in perfect Chinese, "Arise, ye who refuse to be slaves." It is the first line of the Chinese national anthem. The otherwise proud Danish father and Italian mother were also a little worried. Hearing stories about selfless communist heroes, saluting the national Chinese five-star flag and singing 'March of the Volunteers' are everyday activities for a child in Chinese kindergarten. Understandably, foreign parents might not like the sound of this, but it is also becoming more common that Chinese parents seek out alternatives to the official public kindergartens and school system.

The Programme for International Student Assessment (PISA) tests has regularly ranked schools in Shanghai as global number one in reading, science and math (Korea and Hong Kong being second and third). Since then, the Chinese school system has become a "hot potato" in many Western countries. Several TV documentaries, and the accompanying discussions in the media, have appeared where Chinese students competed with students from Western countries. On Danish TV, a show had two ninth grade Chinese and Danish classes competing in several subjects, and the Danish class lost out quite embarrassingly. A BBC show called "Are Our Kids Tough Enough?", where Chinese teachers taught UK school children using Chinese methods, also clearly showed that the more arduous Chinese system has obvious benefits, at least in terms of test results.

There has been a high degree of speculation as to how the Chinese are able to continuously place the Shanghai students on the top of the PISA test. In many Western eyes, the Chinese education system is now seen as a world-class school system, and the envy of Western educators and politicians. Not surprisingly, much of the talk has been about how Western school systems can learn from the Chinese. Discipline in the classroom, the knowledge of how important education is, and respect for the teachers to name a few, are often mentioned as areas where students in the West can improve a lot.

But whereas many in the West look to China for solutions to the problems of our education systems, many Chinese parents I know don't understand why that is. To them, quite the opposite is the case. We have several friends who have started home kindergarten and home schooling for their children, mainly because of how education is taught and thought of in China, but also because of the extreme pressure the system puts on their children. Interestingly, if you stand outside an international school in Beijing in the morning, you will notice from the white license plates on the luxury cars, how many high-ranking Chinese military officials manage to send their offspring to an international school. This goes for party officials as well. It is very clear that the leaders of China don't even want the Chinese education system for their own children, as even the majority of the members of the all powerful Politburo (including Xi Jinping), the supreme decision-making body of a Communist Party increasingly steeped in anti-Western rhetoric, has children and grandchildren educated at universities in the West. The Chinese education system is only for the *jiucai* (Chinese leek), Chinese internet slang, referring to the Chinese masses or someone who can be repeatedly deceived and exploited.

These children taken out of the system will never have to sit the feared *gaokao*, the college entrance examination which will decide their whole future. However, for the very same reason, they are also therefore completely ruled out of the Chinese education system as well as a huge range of job opportunities. Instead, they will most likely have to go abroad for further education after they finish high school. A growing number are now Chinese Christians, who don't want their children to be taught Communist party history and religion in school, and therefore adopt a curriculum from an American Christian school system. Others were trying to create more discussion and even openly rebel from the inside, like the Chinese blogger Han Han, who mocked Chinese education and its focus on tests and memorizing huge amounts of text by comparing it to "standing in the shower wearing a padded coat." It was rather short-lived though. Once celebrated as the voice of China's rebellious youth and the country's most-read blogger, Han Han, soon shifted away from his social and political criticism towards a career as a race car driver, film-making and family life.

But it's not just parents who question the education system. Many school leaders from the exact same high schools which received the highest PISA scores also question both the test results and the way education is taught in China. "A written test says very little about how well young people are prepared to solve complex problems," Zhang Renli, Principal of Jing'An Education College Affiliated School, one of the top schools in Shanghai, was quoted as saying.

Even the students have started to rebel. A 22-year-old university student named Zhong Daoran famously published a book called *I Do Not Forgive*, reflecting a widespread feeling of aversion among many Chinese students. "In elementary school, they rob us of our independent values; in middle school, they take away our capacity for independent thought; and in university, they take away our dreams and idealism. Thus our brains become as empty as the underpants of a eunuch."

This was the situation we were faced with if our sons were to grow up and attend the local Chinese school system. Would it be possible to raise them with the best of both worlds? How to incorporate both the more laissez-faire Danish system emphasizing play and creativity, while at the same time adhering to the Chinese model of discipline, long hours and structured extracurricular activities? Not surprisingly, we are not the only ones who face this dilemma. Amy Chua's book has also been much discussed in China, and a TV series, called Tiger Mom and Cat Dad, even came out taking up many of these serious questions for debate. The popular show dealt with them in a more humorous way when the often conflicting education philosophies of a fierce Tiger Mom who believes that education is a painful process and a chilled-out Cat Dad and his gentle and relaxed approach to children's education colliding as they try to raise their young daughter.

Whether or not the Chinese Tiger Mother and the Chinese way of teaching and educating is superior, as Amy Chua says, I don't know, but I can see great things in both worlds, systems and ways of thinking about learning and education.

It was a huge challenge and a daunting task, and from the outset, I felt the pressure on my shoulders to find the 'right' way. It was a lot more than just a speed bump, and we are always trying to find the middle ground in between a Tiger Mom and a Cat Dad. Most of the time we succeed.

19

UNDER THE INFLUENCE

WHEN MY SISTER had her first child in Denmark, my parents were of course overjoyed. But they did not jump in the car the minute they got the news. They waited eagerly until my sister said she was ready to receive visitors and then they made sure not to overstay their welcome. After that they were probably waiting (impatiently) for an invitation to visit again. For them, it was customary to accept the wishes of my sister and her boyfriend for privacy, and to give them time to learn how to be a mother and father and then how to bring up their little girl. When my parents do come to visit either my sister or us, they will always ask if there is something they can help with as they don't want to intrude in our homes. I think this would be a very typical situation in many Western countries, but it is a very atypical one in China.

Grandparents in China often expect to move in with the happy couple and the grandchild or children and instantly become a "three generations under one roof" kind of family. Traditionally, "Four generations under one roof" has always been the ideal concept of family life for Chinese people, and it symbolizes the ideals of harmony, happiness, longevity, and a large and thriving family. However, in today's China four generations living together has become almost as rare as seeing a panda in the wild.

Statistics show that the average size of a Chinese household has decreased significantly from 5.3 people in 1949 to 3.1 in 2015.

Despite this decline the family ideal of four generations under one roof remains unchanged. Most elderly people in China still live at home instead of in a nursing home; the younger generation considers it their duty to take care of their parents. And on the other hand, which is also clearly visible in all public parks and spaces and our local neighbourhood, Chinese grandparents think it is their right and responsibility to look after the grandchildren. Not only look after, in fact, but bring them up. They would usually not ask permission from the parents to scold or correct their grandchildren. It is their right to do so.

My Australian friend Juliana lives with her Chinese husband, their three-year old son, and his parents in an apartment in northern Beijing, close to the 2008 Beijing National Stadium, the Bird's Nest. She told me that while it was great to know that there would always be caring grandparents around if she or her husband had to stay out a little later for work, and know that her son would never be the last kid in pre-kindergarten to be picked up, it took quite a number of discussions and everyday small battles over what would be the "right" way to raise her son. On one hand, her in-laws always say that they would not interfere in the way she and her husband chose to bring up their son, but it just didn't work like that in reality. The biggest problem for her is also a problem for the majority of all other Chinese parents with little children. Grandparents and/or younger female relatives have always taken care of young children. In her case, it means that her husband was brought up by his grandmother and a young female relative, but not by his parents who were busy with their careers. In her words, her in-laws have never really tried being parents, so even though they are lovely grandparents, spoiling their grandson like all other grandparents, in reality they don't have much of an idea of what to do and what parenting means.

Don't get me wrong. To have grandparents around is wonderful, both for you and for your children, and I do wish that both Fu's and my parents lived closer to us. But the way it sometimes works out in China can be overwhelming and rather difficult to deal with for a foreigner married to a Chinese person, especially if the in-laws move in with you. No doubt that generational problems exist everywhere, all over the world. But the speed with which Chinese society has changed in the last thirty years has made the generation gap between couples born in the 1980s and their parents born in the 1950s or 1960s, very wide indeed. And old mind-sets die hard.

In the early 1980's when our Chinese friend Hong grew up in Shandong, she was looked after by her grandmother after her parents had left to work in another city. Naturally, according to her grandmother at least, there came a time when it was time to start binding Hong's little feet, so she could grow up with beautiful small lily feet and potentially find a wealthy husband. Her grandmother started by tightly wrapping bandages around them to stop any natural growth, and then Hong could expect to go through years of excruciating pain, until the process had finished and her grandmother was satisfied with the result. Luckily for Hong, her parents came back to visit and of course immediately stopped the grandmother. But her feet will never be completely normal again.

One nice sunny spring afternoon, in our compound, another grandmother was out with her granddaughter, pushing her in a stroller. The cute little girl was one year and two months old and her pants had been sewn in so her feet were stuck inside the pants. The grandmother explained, as the most natural thing, that the girl was not allowed to stand up. She could sit on the floor, they would carry her around, or she would sit in her stroller, but not once was she allowed to try walking. We were a little baffled, to say the least, at this odd behaviour. Apparently the idea behind it was that, in this way the girl would not grow up to be bow-legged, but would have desirable straight legs befitting a pretty girl. I am still not clear on how that would be the outcome, but afterwards when I talked to more Chinese people about this, many confirmed (and not only grandmothers) that this is a non-negotiable fact, both scientifically and medically proven.

Another proud grandmother of a set of twin boys in our compound told Fu that she gives the boys Chinese medicine everyday whether they are sick or not. She strongly believes that it will prevent them from becoming sick altogether. Clearly it has not worked, as they were sick all through that winter, and if that was not enough, their teeth were all black because of the overuse of medicine.

Even though these stories verge on the extreme, it says a lot about how long it can take for superstitions and old customs to die out with such a generational gap, despite endless campaigns up through the twentieth century and a large rise in the general education level in China.

I have only lived with my in-laws, or I should say "baba mama", up to three weeks at a time, so I do not really count. And the biggest issue I have with my mother-in-law when we visit is probably that even though I know that she shows her love for us by cooking huge meals with tons of meat and washing our clothes as a way of saying 'I love you', I wish that once in while she would rather say those words instead.

But an American friend of mine lives with his Chinese wife, their son, and his in-laws. He told me their story. First of all, he and his wife are 25 years apart. She became pregnant even before they were married and neither his nor her parents approved of the relationship, even less a marriage. She went back to visit her parents for Chinese New Year just after giving birth without taking her son or husband with her and without even telling her parents that she had given birth to a grandson. He had no idea what to do with the little baby boy and saw no other solution than to bring him to Schindler's–the local Beijing German-style pub where the Chinese *fuwuyuan* (waitresses) would take care of the little new-born all day–and this he did every single day until she came back.

His mother-in-law would not give out the *hukou* certificate to his bride-to-be when they finally announced they were getting married. Without the *hukou*, Chinese cannot get married in China. Finally they got it from the father-in-law. Now they live together and he has his in-laws, especially the mother-in-law, who by the way are about the same age as he is, snooping around in his belongings, looking over his shoulder, checking his every move, looking through everything he buys in the local supermarket chain catering to foreigners, and during the hot and humid Beijing summers he sits sweating trying to work in 35-40 degrees Celsius because his in-laws believe that air con is the devil in disguise. They also firmly believe that both air purifiers and air humidifiers are bad, because what will happen when the air inside is nice and clean when it isn't when you step back outside? You will of course become sick. And as he tells me, it is fruitless to try and reason and discuss. These things are set in stone. Not surprisingly he often seems a little stressed when I meet him.

All this being said, it is likely more difficult for a foreign woman to live with her Chinese in-laws under the influence of the mother-in-law. The daughter-in-law–mother-in-law relationship is traditionally much more difficult because traditional Chinese culture holds wives to be subordinate to their mothers-in-law. Being under the influence of the mother-in-law can be tough in China and that story has as long a history as China itself. The daughter-in-law is traditionally seen as an outsider in the family. She is expected to provide grandchildren, demonstrate filial respect and serve the mother-in-law. In the past it was even quite normal to adopt a daughter-in-law when she was still a child in order for the future mother-in-law to raise a perfect, hardworking and obedient daughter- in-law. But how odd it must have been for the children to grow up as brother and sister and then all of a sudden be married as husband and wife.

Thus women who suffered long and hard under their mother in-laws' thumbs look forward to the day when they can rule their sons' wives with the same heavy hand. They expect to dictate how their daughters-in-law cook, clean, shop, educate the grandchildren and even over how they dress and wear makeup.

The importance of the mother-in-law and the difficulties it brings with it into married life, is clear from this comment on Chinese social media:

"It's the middle of the night and a husband and wife are arguing. The husband shouts three times: "because she is my mother, because she is my mother, because she is my mother." The mother-daughter-in-law relationship is, for the Chinese people, a 5,000 year old eternally beautiful landscape!

20

THE LONG MARCH

EVERY NIGHT on my way to the nightly toilet visit (yes, I was already that old!), I tried to be as silent as a mouse tiptoeing past a sleeping pack of hungry hyenas who always seem to sleep with one eye open. In reality, I just needed to pass a sleeping baby of not yet nine months and completely toothless, but it seemed to be equally as dangerous, and the chance he would wake up and scream louder than the hyenas and wake up the rest of the family, was ever-present. Just one foot misplaced in the darkness decided whether this trip would be a success or a disastrous failure. Stepping on a piece of LEGO left by Luka or Louis (I am a huge fan of LEGO, just not when I step on it in bare feet), and I was dead meat.

Don't get me wrong. It is an indescribable joy to become a father and see your children smile at you every day and come running to you and give you a hug when you come home from work. Although I did wonder sometimes when Luka comes running at full speed with one of his big dinosaur toys (made in Germany and therefore heavy) and hits me right in the balls. Doubled over in pain, I look at him and mumble that there is definitely not a chance in the world now that he will get a little sister. But you still forgive him, because he is just standing there in innocent bewilderment saying *"baba kule"*: daddy is crying.

THE LONG MARCH

Especially because Luka's first words were *"baba"*.

Because that is what nearly every Chinese we meet will at some point ask: Why don't you get a number three? Then they say, "Why don't you get a sweet little girl?" And then come the "statistics": Number one: If the boy looks a little like a girl the next child will be a girl (and Louis does indeed look a little like a girl). Number two: Look at how many fingers the brothers are sucking and you will know whether the next child will be a boy or girl. Luka was sucking on one finger, thus next in line was a boy, but Louis was sucking on two fingers, and then, according to folklore, we would be blessed by a girl if we should decide to try for a number three.

I was even so proud of being a father, that when I found a T-shirt in a shop across from the birth place of the famous Chinese writer Lu Xun, saying *"jiao baba"* meaning "call me dad", that I didn't think twice before I bought it. Only later, Fu told me that it is a common saying about guys who have a girl in every port or city from Hong Kong to Harbin...Slightly embarrassing.

It seemed like only yesterday that Fu gave birth to Luka, but Luka was already a little boy of nearly four and Louis had just turned one, and they were both charming all the old ladies in our compound. Our compound was full of sweet old ladies (at least semi-sweet), or at least I thought so. Semi because they were all members of the local evening performance troupe, dancing in almost perfect synchrony, to Chinese pop, disco or techno music, at an ear-splitting volume, as well as the 'clap-your-hands mafia', as we call them, because they walked, most often backwards, for what felt like hours every morning continuously clapping their hands together (most often out of step), clapping on their buttocks, and heads, pretty much everywhere, occasionally stopping to shout at a tree trunk, all for supposed health benefits, but more likely to deprive me of my precious morning sleep. I wonder if it was a continuation of the age-old tradition of old Beijing police officers who coordinated their beats in the city's *hutong* (alleyways) for hundreds of years by clapping large pieces of hollow bamboo together, also in much the same way, depriving all residents, but especially visiting foreigners who were not used to it, of their night's sleep, as old accounts reveal. I am sure it was a conspiracy.

Right about when the first draft this book was nearly finished, we had to take the very difficult decision whether or not to stay in China. Living and working in China had been my dream, and I truly fell in love with Beijing, both the city and its people. I had also married and started a family here. As one of the ultimate signs of having settled down in China and in a sense maybe becoming and acting more and more like a Chinese, I started noticing that quite often people, Chinese as well as other foreigners, would ask me if I had any Chinese ancestry (maybe there really is some Genghis Khan deep down in there, and China considers Genghis Chinese anyway). I had been lucky and privileged to be part of several start-up projects and businesses, (not least my own *Beijing Postcards*) and had worked as a freelance journalist, writer, as well as in expat insurance, and in the travel industry, among others, and I had made a decent income. However, I had, until now, postponed unpleasant thoughts of savings and pensions. But I was now in my late thirties, and I had to be a realist.

Having a family and raising children in China can be a costly affair and prices were going up all the time. At the same time, in early 2013, pollution levels also skyrocketed across northern China (WHO said that any number above 25 on the pollution scale would be a health risk. In Beijing it would often climb up over 900), and both our boys were suffering for months with asthma and bronchitis, many days wheezing like two old men. It was very time-consuming both literally and psychologically, and for days we mostly kept the boys indoors and shut all windows and switched on the air purifiers on maximum strength. I also had to admit to myself that while I was never without my anti-pollution mask on my bike, I often woke up coughing like an old-time seasoned smoker, although I have never smoked in my life.

In May, 2013, even the *China Daily* reported that Beijing and all other first-tier cities in mainland China, were barely suitable for living and Beijing ranked only 119th in ecological environment terms. Finally, one day, when a friend sent me a snapshot from his children's international school in Beijing of a sign saying: "Please do not open the window. Let's keep the indoor air clean", I had to ask myself if this was a price I wanted to pay for staying in my beloved Beijing. No, not really, was the answer. But it was still a decision that would change our lives completely and thus not one to be taken overnight.

During the Long March (1934-35), Mao Zedong and his communist compatriots completed a gruelling 9,000 km from southeastern Jiangxi, through some of China's most difficult mountainous terrain, finally ending up in northern Shaanxi Province, and now the idea slowly formed that it would be a wise decision to set out on our own arduous Long March and move to Denmark. The date for our departure was set for July 14, 2013. However, there was one rather big problem that we would have to deal with first; otherwise we would have to leave a quarter of the family behind in China.

Remember where we left off last time, with Louis? Well now is the time to go back and finish the tale, because even though we were ready to leave China, we simply couldn't. Louis was still

Chinese and we had already used up the only exit permit he was allowed and given. He would simply not be allowed to leave the country. The renunciation of his Chinese citizenship had not gone through yet, despite the fact that it had already taken more than ten months. A phone call to Captain Li at the PSB in Chengdu to ask for an update of the progress of his case, got us nowhere. All we could do was wait. Despite the bleak prospects, we decided to go to Chengdu again anyway to see whether or not anything could be done on the spot.

Arriving in Chengdu, we went to talk to Captain Li. Finally, smiling at us while chewing on the end of his filterless Pride cigarette between his lips, he told us he had come up with *the* solution. We could solve the problem by officially giving Louis a Chinese *hukou* certificate and then apply for a Chinese passport. Then we could go to the Danish embassy and apply for a visa to go to Denmark. Then, after that, if we still wanted to, we could start the application process to renounce his Chinese citizenship once more.

As mentioned before, we had already learned that such a solution would probably cost us somewhere around 100,000-120,000 RMB to officially register Louis with a *hukou*. Then you start to ask yourself: Does he really need it, and if so, why? What are the benefits?

The only real benefit we could see was that with the Chinese nationality and *hukou* he would be able to attend a cheaper local Chinese school for Chinese nationals only. On the other hand, it would be a hassle every time we wanted to leave China as we would have to not only apply for a visa, but we would also often have to make a deposit of up to 100,000 RMB in order for the visa application to go through. The conclusion was that since we were planning to leave China, it did not make much sense to do it.

THE LONG MARCH

Was there really no other way?

Having lived in China for many years, I knew one thing. There was bound to be another solution of some sorts. I started making phone calls to pretty much anyone I could imagine who might have contacts to visa agents of the more grey variety. In the past, Chinese visas and visa problems, just like my own, could nearly always be handled by a visa agent with the right contacts in the right places. But I quickly came to realize that this was not the case anymore. It seemed like this door had long-since closed. We then started to ask around and make internet searches on how much it would cost if we just showed up in the airport with a six-month overstayed Chinese tourist visa in Louis' Danish passport. We could not find any clear answers here either, but we found that overstayed visas were often rewarded with large fines and sometimes even detention.

To be honest, we were at a loss and felt rather helpless. We had three weeks left before we had to leave China, but still we had found no solution to Louis' citizenship problem. The day before we had planned to go back to Beijing to do our final goodbyes and pack up our stuff, we received yet another phone call from Captain Li from the PSB. This time he had come up with a new, doable and much cheaper solution. If we signed a paper promising that we would never ever ask for an extra entry-exit permit for Louis, the PSB would extraordinarily grant Louis an extra exit permit to leave China. Finally, a solution which would work. We were overjoyed and of course immediately went to sign the papers to get the paperwork in order.

We were finally ready to leave China–all of us, however Louis' nationality problem was never actually solved while we were in China.

Epilogue

Made in Denmark

WE NOW LIVE in Denmark, and we enjoy life here with all the 'huegah', the cosiness and a whole lot of candles, remember? But of course we miss Beijing and China. We miss the atmosphere, the energy, the spontaneousness, the people, and even the noise sometimes, but primarily we miss family, friends and food, mostly in that order, and Chinese restaurants in Denmark are in general unfortunately really not very good. Luckily I married a true kitchen goddess.

We also had to get used to many other daily challenges.

First of all, I had to stop greeting friends and colleagues with "You have gained weight", when they had been away on holiday. We had to teach Luka that it was not okay anymore just to take off his pants whenever he wanted to pee. Fu had to learn to stop asking the teacher what number Luka is in his class at the parent school meetings and get used to the doctors advice here most of the time is a simple "drink hot tea and take a painkiller". I had to get used to colleagues looking at me in disbelief whenever I drink scolding hot water on a warm summer day, or when I, without even giving it a second thought, spit my bones out on the table next to my plate, or loudly slurp my noodle soup.

I also had to get used to utter silence. Provincial life in a city in Denmark is really quiet. Take a walk almost anywhere on a

MADE IN DENMARK

Sunday (actually, pretty much any day), and you cannot help but think: where is everyone? Sometimes I wake up early in the morning and wonder if something is wrong, because there is not a single sound to be heard. During the winter months, the neighbourhood is so still that it seems as if all Danes are in hibernation. I must admit that once in a while I do miss the sounds of the dancing and clapping old ladies in our compound and all the other familiar sounds and noises emanating from our Beijing neighbourhood. On the other hand, one of the benefits of moving to Denmark has been that I am now able to buy a shirt which will fit me just fine with only one X or none at all, instead of up to 7 x XL which is my T-shirt size record in China.

There were also other things I had to get used to. In the first few years in China, I would often say hello to someone I met on the street, only to quickly realize that I had never met the person before in my life. It might sound stupid, I know, but during the first few years I often had a hard time differentiating Chinese people. I had the exact same feeling the first few months after we moved back to Denmark. Just like the Chinese would say, all foreigners look the same.

We also had to get used to an even more rigid and slow bureaucracy, in many respects. And although we ended up living on the fourth floor in our last apartment in Beijing, we couldn't completely disregard the Chinese belief in lucky and unlucky numbers, and I wanted Fu to have the best welcome and start in her new life in Denmark. And a Danish ID number is the place to start.

After waiting for what seemed like an eternity, Fu's residence permit came through. With this, she also received an official Danish social security number. Guess what! I think the Danish immigration authorities could use a little course in cultural understanding and sensitivity. The number ends in numerous 4's and 9's, translating into something like "die, die, a slow death". I just thank God we are not that superstitious, but could I just please have some '8's' in there somewhere?

Efforts by both the Nationalist and the Communist governments to eradicate superstitious beliefs in Chinese society in an effort to modernize the country have been in large part unsuccessful. Today people still go to fortune tellers to find a good date to get married, have a baby or find a lucky name for the baby, still believe in lucky and unlucky numbers and still hang or place protective buddhas, bodhisattvas, posters and talismans, sometimes in the form of Chairman Mao as "the red sun in our heart" or even a President Xi Jinping charm or, literally, his head on a platter, in their cars and homes. These beliefs allow Chinese people to maintain some sense of control over their fates as the country undergoes tumultuous social and economic changes.

I am happy to say that Fu became pregnant again. This time made in Denmark. And contrary to what all our Danish friends have told us, "you already have two boys so number three will also be a boy," we started buying pink clothes. Louis and the Chinese folklore was right once again. Two fingers it was, and it was a girl. So far it will be three, and despite what the sweet elderly soothsayer with a black turban and long dangling earrings proclaimed, I think I will call it a day.

Whether or not we will move back to China in the future, I don't know. Who knows, maybe I will one day be back among those disco-dancing and hand clapping retirees walking backwards in a local Beijing neighborhood.

BIBLIOGRAPHY

In writing this book, most of the material came from my own personal experiences, and those of friends, family members and acquaintances, but I also consulted other books, articles and websites. Here is a selection you might find interesting:

Baby Gender Predictor (2011). http://babygender-predictor.blogspot.com/2011/12/chinese-baby-calendar.html

Gao, Ying, Zhang, Xiulan & Zhu, Weilong (2013). "A Study on Cross-Nation Marriages of Beijing" (CHI). *Renkou yu Jingji* (Population and Economics), No. 1, pp. 27-36.

Jeffreys, Elaine and Wang Pan (2013). 'The Rise of Chinese-Foreign Marriage in Mainland China (1979–2010)', *China Information*, 27, 3: 347–69

Lee, Dominic T. et al (2009). "Antenatal taboos among Chinese women in Hong Kong". *Midwifery*. April 25 (2), pp. 104-113.

Lee, Hyangsook & Edzard Ernst (2004). "Acupuncture for labor pain management: A systematic review". *American Journal of Obstetrics and Gynecology*, Volume 191, Issue 5, November, pp. 1573-1579

Sohu (2015). "Which nationality does Chinese girls love to marry?" (CHI). *Sohu*. https://m.sohu.com/n/426644230/?wscrid=89702_3

Yang, Kaiheng (2020). "A Preliminary Study on the National Differences of the Target Countries of Chinese Foreign Marriages" (CHI). https://www.sohu.com/a/377268608_99906585

Yang, Kaiheng & Zhang Chengcen (2019). "Behind the praise and demeanor: Visual analysis of China's foreign marriage statistics" (CHI). *Sohu*. https://www.sohu.com/a/355976155_99906585

About The Author

Simon Rom Gjeroe is a self-confessed nerd when it comes to China and everything Chinese. He has been interested in China since he saw the movie "The Last Emperor" as a thirteen-year old. During his Chinese studies, he spent two years at Sichuan University in Chengdu, where he lived from 1995 to 1998. That is where he also met his future wife, Fu. After graduating in Chinese and Modern East Asian Studies, he moved to Beijing for work, and, after a few years, also married and settled down with Fu and eventually became the proud father of two boys here. A fluent Mandarin speaker, he has lived in China for more than a decade. He has written articles and books on Chinese travel, food, culture, history and politics. This is his third book. He now lives in Denmark with his family, now including one made in Denmark. He teaches Chinese Studies and History.

www.ingramcontent.com/pod-product-compliance
Lightning Source LLC
LaVergne TN
LVHW030321070526
838199LV00069B/6522